Knitting for Children

Knitting for Children

35 simple knits kids will love to make!

Claire Montgomerie

CICO BOOKS

LONDON NEW YORK

This edition published in 2017 by CICO Books
An imprint of Ryland Peters & Small Ltd
20–21 Jockey's Fields, London WC1R 4BW
341 E 116th St, New York, NY 10029

www.rylandpeters.com

10 9 8 7 6 5 4 3 2 1

First published in 2010 by CICO Books

A CIP catalog record for this book is
available from the Library of Congress and
the British Library.

ISBN: 978 1 78249 461 4

Printed in China

Editor: Kate Haxell
Designer: Elizabeth Healey
Photographers: Terry Benson, Martin Norris,
    and Ian Boddy
Stylists: Emma Hardy and Rose Hammick

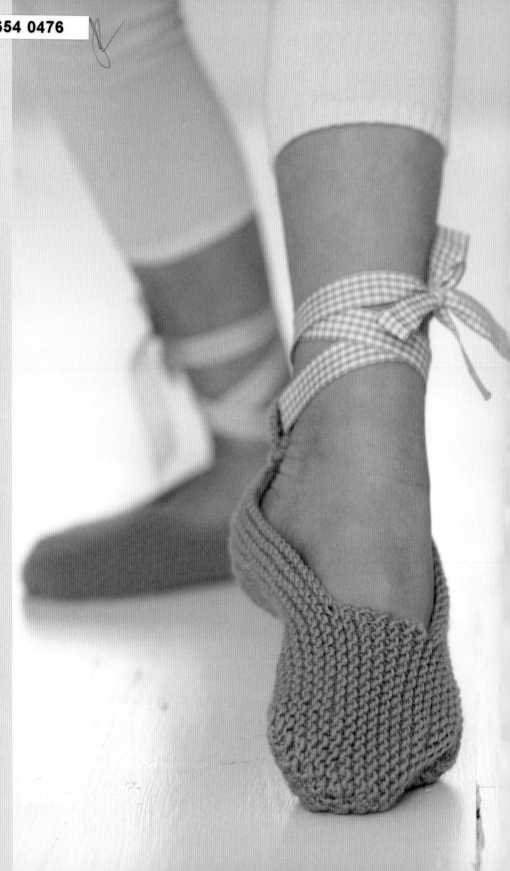

Contents

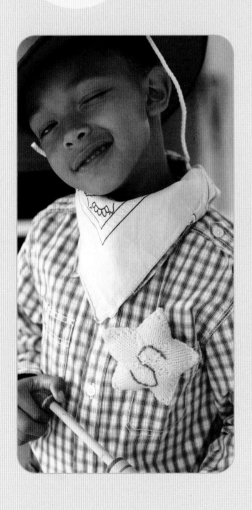

Introduction

There are many reasons to learn to knit, especially as a child. The craft of knitting is not only a fun pastime, it can also be beneficial to children's development. Knitting involves a lot of counting and simple math, as well as being a relaxing and therapeutic occupation, which means that it can aid learning and concentration in some children, especially in those with learning difficulties or attention disorders.

However, knitting books aimed specifically at children are hard to find and one thing that I have discovered through running kids' knitting workshops is that teaching a child to knit is very different from teaching an adult. I have often found that adult-specific knitting books are too complicated or boring for youngsters, yet ones aimed at children are just too simple or babyish, which can discourage them from taking up the craft. Although teaching kids is different from teaching adults, children can most definitely cope with quite challenging patterns, in fact this will help to hold their interest. My experiences have led me to aim to write an interesting, informative, and fun book, aimed solely at children, with lots of alluringly colorful patterns to hold their interest.

I believe that anyone can learn to knit; all it takes is practice and perseverance, but not all children want to commit themselves. However, many of the projects in this book are so small and simple that I hope they will be keen to move onto the next one, and will not even realize that they are progressing through the techniques. Patterns have different skill levels and use the techniques the child will be learning in an interesting yet repetitive way, so they do not know that they are effectively "swatching"— as an adult would do—while they learn.

I have chosen yarns that are easy to use and often formulated especially for children, utilizing a mix of natural fibers to ensure they are kind to young, sensitive skin and man-made fibers to make them durable and easy to wash and care for. However, I have also suggested alternatives so you and your child can play with the look of the projects and use remnants or yarns that are to hand, as many of the patterns use very small amounts of yarn.

Before you dive into the patterns, please do take the time to read my tips on teaching your child to knit (pages 8–11), as I hope my hints and tricks will help make the experience enjoyable and ensure the memory is a warm and happy one for all involved. Most important of all, don't forget to have fun!

Claire Montgomerie

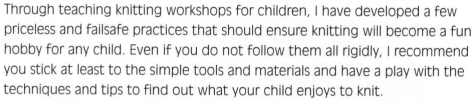

Teaching kids to knit

Through teaching knitting workshops for children, I have developed a few priceless and failsafe practices that should ensure knitting will become a fun hobby for any child. Even if you do not follow them all rigidly, I recommend you stick at least to the simple tools and materials and have a play with the techniques and tips to find out what your child enjoys to knit.

Many people ask me what is the ideal age to teach a child to knit. The truthful answer is "how long is a piece of string?" It really does depend on the child. It is possible for some children to learn the very basics as young as four or five, but this is rare. I have found that the best age is seven or eight, as by this age most children have fully developed motor skills and hand–eye coordination, and can concentrate for longer periods of time. They will also be more likely to take all the techniques in and adopt knitting as a hobby and skill that they will never lose.

Another common question is about which tools to choose. Most people instinctively reach for the larger needles when teaching children, but even for adults large needles can be unwieldy and uncomfortable to use, while children's hands are just too small to cope. Choose size US 6–10 (4–6mm) needles, of a length that is manageable—7½–10in (18–25cm) long is great. You can find needles especially for children that are extra-short with smiley face or patterned decorations, or made from brightly colored plastic, all of which should make them instantly desirable to the young eye.

Choose smooth and stretchy yarn such as wool or acrylic, or a mixture of either of these with other fibers. Don't try fancy yarns at the start, as they may be forgiving when it comes to hiding mistakes, but they may also cause errors through snagging and lack of definition in the stitches.

It is very helpful to cast on for a child and knit a few rows before showing them how to do it themselves, as it is much easier for them to work into a row than a cast-on edge. It also helps them feel as if they have got going already and won't cause them to become discouraged by the sometimes difficult-to-master cast-on technique. A perfect number to cast on is 20 stitches, enough to be substantial and yet not so many that a child will be overwhelmed by each row. It is an easy-to-remember, easy-to-count number that will make it simple to tell if the child has gained or lost stitches and help them to spot their mistakes. If they are having some difficulties with their counting, this will help them with those at the same time.

Go slowly with your child at first, they are generally happy just playing with the yarn and techniques—make the learning like a game. Try to vary the activity as you teach, so have pompom makers and French knitters to hand to embellish the knitting and break up the monotony of knit stitch, especially when you notice any concentration lapses. Don't make them knit for too long. It is a repetitive skill that can cause an ache in the hands of an unpracticed knitter. Short, fun lessons with breaks in between will prevent children from feeling that they are being forced to knit and will make them look forward to picking up the knitting again. You do not have to knit every day, so long as you knit regularly. Perhaps you can find time to knit during a favorite cartoon or before bedtime to unwind. Maybe Saturday evenings will be knitting time. Any quality time with mom, dad or grandma will be eagerly anticipated and if you include all your children in some way, or even their friends, they will want to do it more as it will feel more like a group activity and will be something they can share and talk about.

Have patience with your child; it seems patronising to say so, but sometimes, after a long day together, a parent can be less patient with his or her own child, especially if they really want them to share in the love of

something dear to them. Even if a child's work is a terrible mess, never rip it back as this can undermine their confidence in their ability. Let them see their progression from wonky, and perhaps holey, to beautiful, even knitting. Children often end up with little upside down triangles of knitting, which are caused by increasing many stitches through making unplanned holes and messing up the first stitch of the row. If this happens, don't rip back, but show them how to decrease some stitches by knitting two together so they don't end up getting bored by knitting across a really long row.

Finally, the best tip I can give you is to make it fun! While an adult will happily spend hours knitting swatches that will eventually go either into the bin or a reference file, children want to know what they are making and see the results quite quickly or they may lose interest. Therefore, small projects such as a change purse or mp3 cover are preferable to that standard adult beginner project, the scarf. If it has to be a scarf, make it a mini version for their teddy or doll: perhaps you can make a similar one for your child at the same time so they can dress their toys to match their own outfit and so that you can knit something together.

Knitting should always be relaxing and fun, otherwise, what's the point? So just ensure you both enjoy the process and do not put too much emphasis on perfectly finished knitting. Be flexible and encourage your child to use their imagination; projects can evolve as they are knitted, developing into a final piece that is dictated by the shape of the fabric. Every child is unique and they have a very different view of the world to adults, so let them form fabulous creations from their fabrics, and perhaps, in return, they can also teach you a thing or two about knitting!

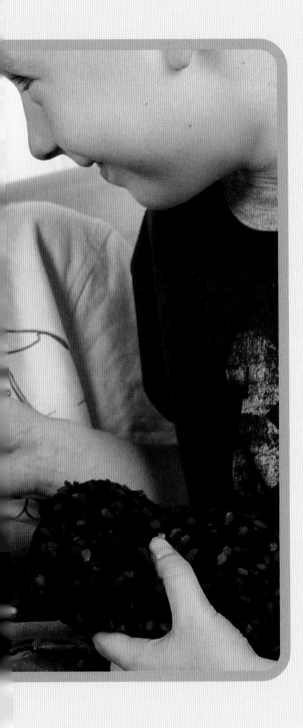

Techniques

Tools

To start with all you need are knitting needles and some yarn, but there are other things you might want to get as you do more knitting.

▽ Knitting needles come in different materials and colors. The color makes no difference, but the material does. Try using bamboo needles at first, because the yarn tends to slip around less on these.

△ There are lots and lots of different colors and types of yarn to choose from.

▽ Stitch holders are used when you need to set some stitches aside to come back to later.

△ Point protectors slip onto the tips of the needles when you are not knitting and stop your stitches falling off. They also stop the needles making holes in your knitting bag.

▷ Some yarns are very strong, you'll need scissors to cut them.

▷ Thick pins are best for holding bits of knitting together when you sew them up.

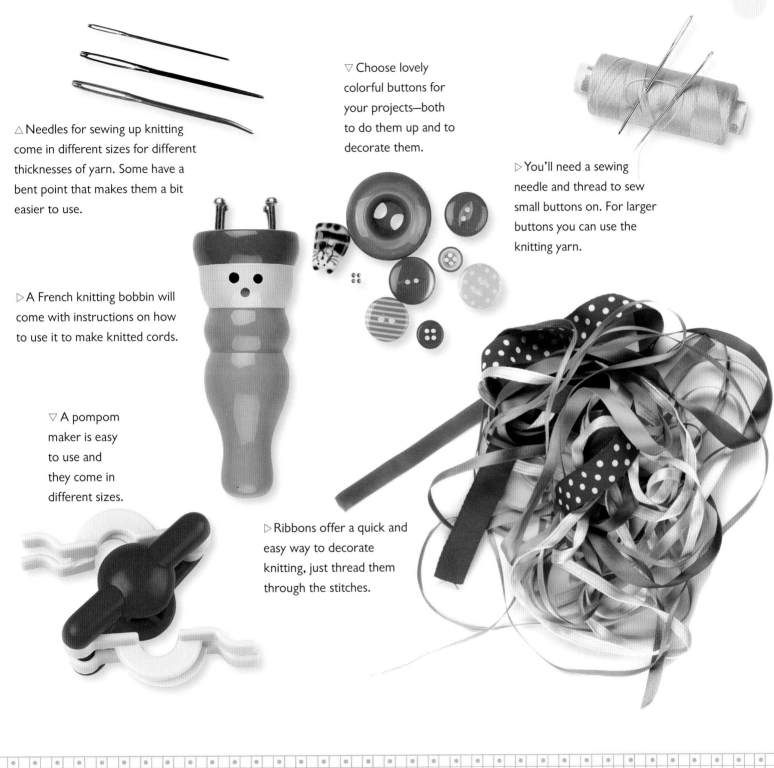

△ Needles for sewing up knitting come in different sizes for different thicknesses of yarn. Some have a bent point that makes them a bit easier to use.

▽ Choose lovely colorful buttons for your projects—both to do them up and to decorate them.

▷ You'll need a sewing needle and thread to sew small buttons on. For larger buttons you can use the knitting yarn.

▷ A French knitting bobbin will come with instructions on how to use it to make knitted cords.

▽ A pompom maker is easy to use and they come in different sizes.

▷ Ribbons offer a quick and easy way to decorate knitting, just thread them through the stitches.

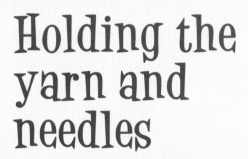

Holding the yarn and needles

There is no one correct way to hold the yarn and needles, everyone finds their own comfortable position, but if you follow my suggestions, you will find it easier to keep an even gauge (tension) when knitting.

There are two most common ways of holding the needles: like a pen or like a knife.

You can hold each needle in the same way, or have each hand use a different way.

Remember that even if you are left-handed you can knit like this, as both hands do some work. However, "lefties" may find continental style easier because the yarn is held in the left hand.

Holding the yarn English style

In English-style knitting, the yarn is held in the right hand.

The ball end of the yarn is wrapped around the right-hand little finger in order to control the amount and speed of yarn feeding through from the ball, and so to control the gauge (tension) of the work (see page 23). The yarn then passes under the two middle fingers and over the pointing finger, which helps to "flick" the yarn around the needle as you knit. If this is too hard at first, you can simply grip the yarn with the right hand and "throw" it round the needle.

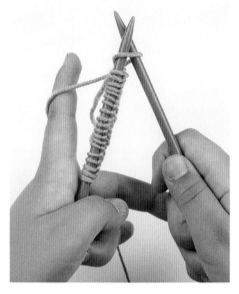

Holding the yarn continental style

Wrap the yarn around the little or middle finger of the left hand, then pass it over the pointing finger of the same hand to hold the yarn taut. Some people like to wrap the yarn just around their pointing finger a few times, but this can cause a tight knitting gauge (tension).

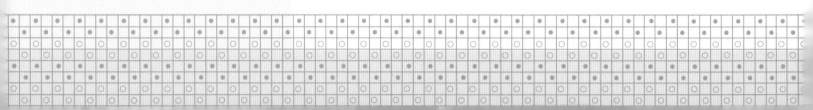

Slip knot and cast on

There are many ways to cast on, but for beginners this is the simplest way, so use this to start with—you can progress to something harder once you have mastered knitting. The first step is to make a slip knot, which will also be your first stitch.

When you are knitting, the yarn leading to the ball is called the "ball-end" of the yarn.

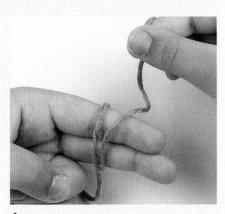

1 Front to back, wind the yarn around two fingers twice to make two loops.

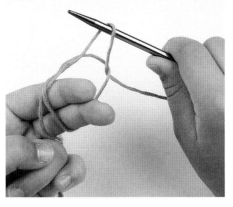

2 Slip a kitting needle under the first loop and hook the second loop through the first one using the tip of the needle.

3 Pull on the ends of the yarn to make the slip knot tight on the needle.

4 You have made your first stitch.

5 Holding the needle in your right hand, make a loop around your left thumb with the ball-end of the yarn.

6 Slip the needle under the loop.

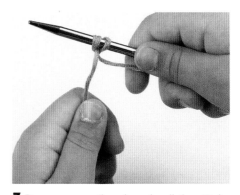

7 Remove your thumb and pull the stitch tight on the needle.

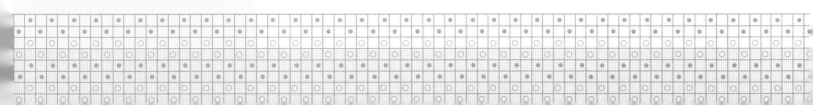

Knit stitch

There are only two stitches in knitting, knit stitch and purl stitch: so there isn't very much to learn!

The knit stitch is the simplest of all stitches. To practice, cast on some stitches and then you can knit every row until you feel you have learned the basic technique.

Knitting every row forms the ridged fabric called garter stitch, which is the simplest stitch pattern (see page 24).

Stockinette (stocking) stitch pattern is made by working one row of knit stitch and one row of purl stitch (see page 20) alternately throughout the fabric.

The aim is to hold the needle with the stitches on in your left hand and the empty needle in your right hand, and to transfer all stitches onto the right-hand needle by knitting a row.

English style

1 Insert the tip of the right-hand needle into the next stitch on the left-hand needle, from the left side of the stitch so that you are going from the front to the back of the knitting.

2 Holding the ball-end of the yarn at the back of the knitting, wrap this yarn around the right-hand needle with your right hand, passing the yarn underneath then over the point of the right-hand needle.

3 Bring a loop of yarn through the stitch on the left-hand needle.

4 Slip the loop off the left-hand needle to complete the stitch, which is now on your right-hand needle.

Repeat these steps with each stitch, until all the stitches on the left-hand needle have been transferred to the right-hand needle. This completes the row. To start a new row, swap the needles in your hands so that the stitches are in your left hand and the yarn is in position at the start of the row.

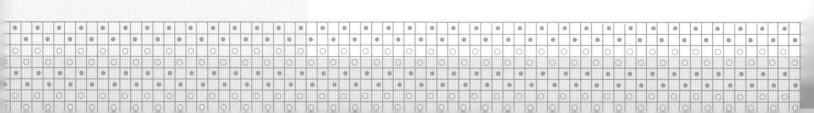

Continental style

1 Insert the tip of the right-hand needle into the next stitch on the left-hand needle, from the left side of the stitch so that you are going from the front to the back of the knitting.

2 Holding the ball-end of the yarn at the back with your left hand, pick this end of the yarn with your right-hand needle.

3 Bring the loop of yarn through the stitch on the left-hand needle.

4 Slip the loop off the left-hand needle to complete the stitch, which is now on your right-hand needle.

Repeat these steps with each stitch, until all the stitches on the left-hand needle have been transferred to the right-hand needle. This completes the row. To start a new row, swap the needles in your hands so that the stitches are in your left hand and the yarn is in position at the start of the row.

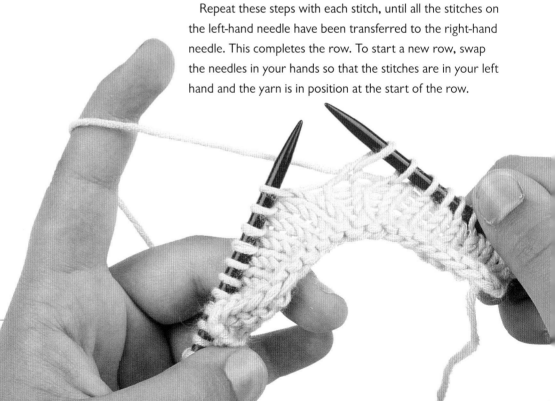

Purl stitch

Most of purl stitch is the other way around to knit stitch. You still hold the needle with stitches on in your left hand, but you insert the right-hand needle a different way into each stitch and you hold the yarn at the front. Work every other row in purl to create stockinette (stocking) stitch (see page 24).

English style

1 Insert the tip of the right-hand needle into the next stitch on the left-hand needle, from the right side of the stitch so that you are going from the back to the front of the knitting.

2 Holding the ball-end of the yarn at the front of the knitting, wrap this yarn around the right-hand needle with your right hand, passing the yarn over and around the right-hand needle.

3 Bring the loop of yarn through the stitch on the left-hand needle.

4 Slip the loop off the left-hand needle to complete the stitch, which is now on your right-hand needle.

Repeat these steps with each stitch, until all the stitches on the left-hand needle have been transferred to the right-hand needle. This completes the row. To start a new row, swap the needles in your hands, so that the yarn is in position at the start of the row, and begin a knit row to make stockinette (stocking) stitch.

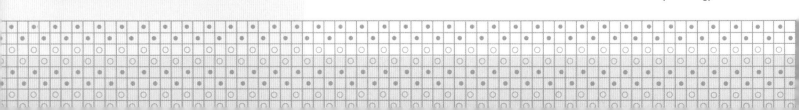

Continental style

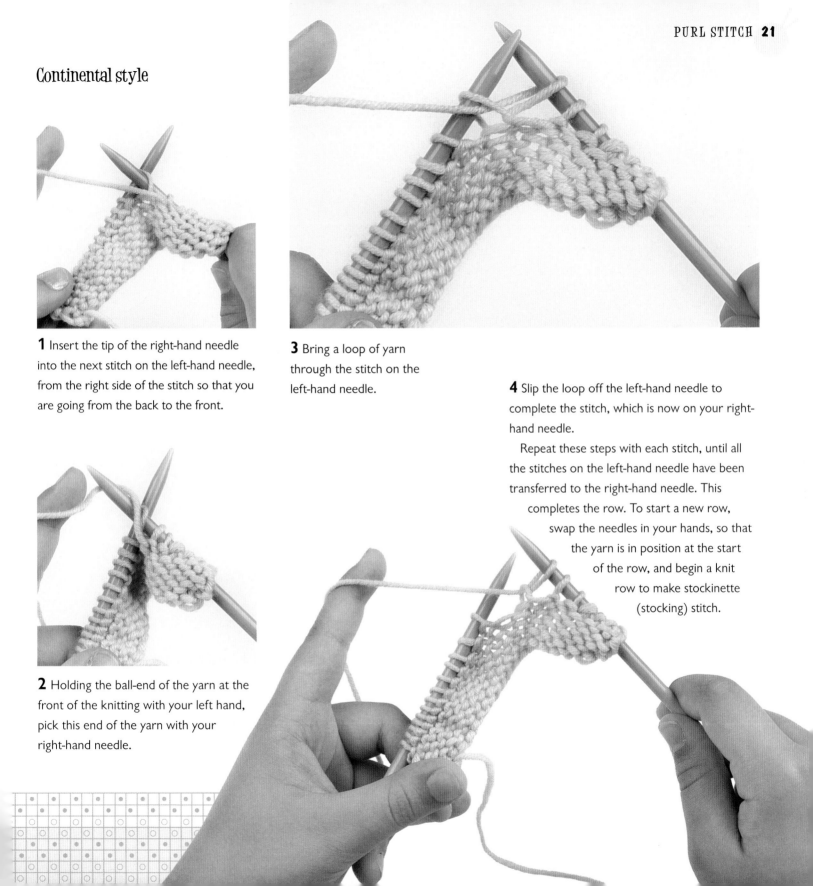

1 Insert the tip of the right-hand needle into the next stitch on the left-hand needle, from the right side of the stitch so that you are going from the back to the front.

2 Holding the ball-end of the yarn at the front of the knitting with your left hand, pick this end of the yarn with your right-hand needle.

3 Bring a loop of yarn through the stitch on the left-hand needle.

4 Slip the loop off the left-hand needle to complete the stitch, which is now on your right-hand needle.

Repeat these steps with each stitch, until all the stitches on the left-hand needle have been transferred to the right-hand needle. This completes the row. To start a new row, swap the needles in your hands, so that the yarn is in position at the start of the row, and begin a knit row to make stockinette (stocking) stitch.

Bind (cast) off

When you have finished knitting you need to bind (cast) off so that all your work doesn't just unravel!

1 First knit two stitches (see page 18).

2 Slip the tip of your left-hand needle into the first stitch you knitted and lift it over the stitch closest to the tip of the needle.

3 Lift the first stitch over the second one and drop it off both needles.

4 Knit one more stitch, so there are two on the right-hand needle again, and repeat all the steps until all you have left is one stitch on the right-hand needle. All the other stitches have been bound (cast) off.

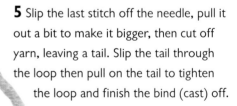

5 Slip the last stitch off the needle, pull it out a bit to make it bigger, then cut off yarn, leaving a tail. Slip the tail through the loop then pull on the tail to tighten the loop and finish the bind (cast) off.

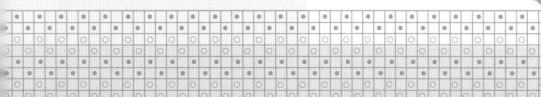

Gauge (tension)

Everybody tends to knit at a different gauge (tension), which means how big or small your stitches are, or how loosely or tightly you knit.

Gauge (tension) varies from knitter to knitter and also when different stitch patterns, yarn fibers, and needle materials are used. The two swatches below have the same number of stitches and rows and were knitted in the same yarn with the same needles, but they were made by two different people. One person has a much looser gauge (tension) than the other, so their swatch is bigger.

A gauge (tension) swatch is used to make sure that you are knitting at the gauge (tension) called for in the pattern. This is essential because the projects are designed to fit certain sizes, so if your gauge (tension) is too loose your project will be too big, and if it is too tight, the project will be too small.

To make a gauge (tension) swatch you need to knit a small square about 4 x 4in (10 x 10cm) in the main yarn and stitch used in the pattern. Lay the swatch flat, place a ruler on it, and count the number of stitches per inch (centimeter).

If you find you have more stitches per inch (centimeter) than asked for in the pattern, then your gauge (tension) is too tight and you need to make it looser. The best way to do this is to increase the size of knitting needle you use until the gauge (tension) is as close as you can get it. If there are fewer stitches than required, then your gauge (tension) is too loose, and you need to decrease the size of knitting needle you use.

Of course, knitting a gauge (tension) swatch takes time and with some small projects where a good fit is not needed, such as some accessories and toys, you do not need to knit a swatch.

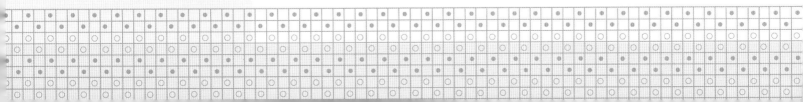

Stitch patterns

Depending on how you combine knit and purl stitches, you can make various stitch patterns to produce knitted fabrics that feel and look very different. These are the four stitch patterns you will find in this book.

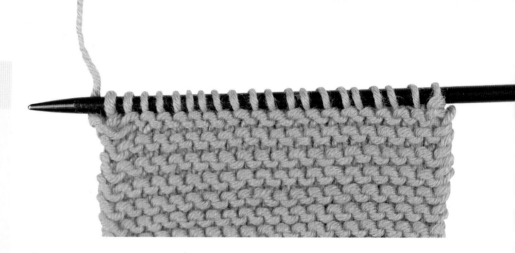

Garter stitch

Knitting every row forms a ridged fabric called garter stitch, which is the simplest stitch pattern. It is the same on both sides and so is a flat, even fabric that is perfect for scarves or edges.

Stockinette (stocking) stitch

This is made by alternately working one row of knit stitch and one row of purl stitch. This makes a fabric that is different on each side. The knit, or plain, side is flat and the stitches look like little "V"s (above left). The purl side is bumpy and textured, with the stitches like little wiggles (above right), and is called reverse stockinette (stocking) stitch.

This fabric curls slightly and so is best used in projects that need to be sewn up, which flattens the curly edges.

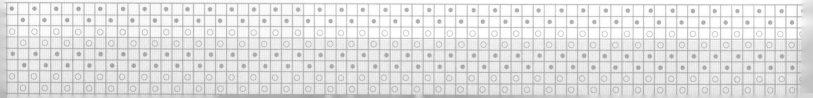

Seed (moss) stitch

Seed (moss) stitch is made by working alternate knit and purl stitches across the same row. As you hold the yarn at the back for knit stitches and at the front for purl stitches, you need to move it after each stitch.

After a knit stitch you must pass the yarn in between the needles to the front of the knitting to work the next purl stitch. After a purl stitch you must pass the yarn in between the needles to the back to make the next knit stitch.

In each row you knit the stitches that were knitted in the last row, and purl those that were purled to create the bumpy texture.

Rib stitch

Rib stitch is created like seed (moss) stitch by working knits and purls alternately across a row. But in each row you knit the stitches that were purled in the last row and vice versa to make the vertical stripes of stitches.

Shaping

To shape a knitted piece you have to increase or decrease the number of stitches on the needles. Here are the simplest ways.

Increasing (inc1)

1 Knit into the front of the next stitch on the left-hand knitting needle, but do not slip it off the needle.

2 With the stitch still on the left-hand needle and the yarn at the back, knit into the back of the same stitch and then slip it off the needle.

3 You have made one stitch into two stitches and so increased by one.

Decreasing (k2tog)

1 Insert the right-hand needle through the fronts of the second then the first stitches on the left-hand needle, from left to right.

2 Then knit the two stitches together, knitting in the usual way (see page 18), and slide both from the left-hand needle.

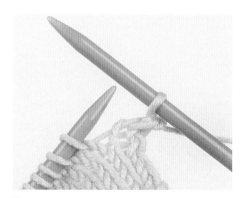

3 You have made two stitches into one stitch and so decreased by one.

Yarnover (yo)

Wrapping the yarn over the needle creates a small hole in the work and an extra stitch. If you only want the hole and not an increase, you must knit two together to decrease (see opposite) straight after the yo.

1 Bring the yarn forward between the needles, then take it over the right-hand needle and hold it at the back.

2 Knit the next stitch. Work in pattern to the end of the row.

3 On the next row, purl into the loop of the yo as if it were a normal stitch and continue in pattern to the end of the row.

4 Where you made the yo, a small hole is formed, perfect for threading a ribbon through or as a little buttonhole.

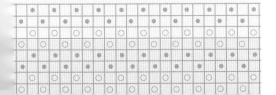

Changing color

When you want to make striped fabrics, or you run out of a ball of yarn, you need to add a new ball at the beginning of the row.

1 Tie the new yarn around the tail of the old yarn, keeping the knot loose.

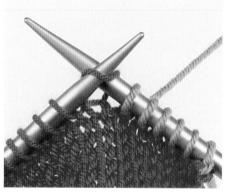

2 Push the knot up next to stitches the pull it tight. Work the next row using the new yarn.

Picking up stitches

Sometimes you need to work a neat edge along the side of a fabric you have already knitted, which is why you need to know how to make the first line of stitches for this edge: this is called picking up stitches. Always do this with the right side of the fabric facing you and try to space the stitches you pick up at equal intervals.

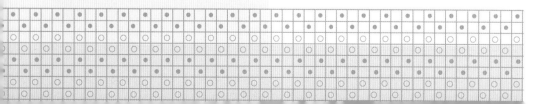
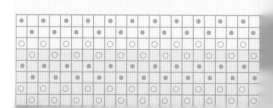

1 Hold the needle in your right hand and insert it through the fabric from front to back where you want to pick up the stitch.

2 Wrap a new piece of yarn around the needle, as if to knit a stitch.

3 Pull the loop through the knitted fabric to the front. Continue in this way along the edge until all the stitches are picked up. Work on these stitches as instructed in the pattern.

Sewing up

Sewing up knitting can be done in many ways, but using a whip stitch is the easiest. However, you can see the stitches quite easily so sometimes it is nice to make a feature of this by using a different color yarn to the one used in the project.

1 Secure the yarn to one piece of fabric with a few little stitches on the back. Lay the pieces to be joined next to each other, right sides up. Insert the needle into the front of one piece of fabric, then up from the back of the adjoining fabric.

2 Repeat along the seam.

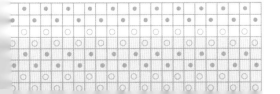

Pompoms

Pompoms are so simple to make. You can make them from rings of cardboard, but buying a plastic pompom maker is so much quicker and simpler, and you don't have to make a new one each time you want to make pompoms. You can buy makers in all shapes and sizes—even heart shaped!

Some types work a little differently to the one shown, so always read the instructions on the pack before you start.

Here is a little tip: try cutting the end of the yarn for tying before you begin so that you don't have to put down the pompom maker in the middle of cutting the pompom.

1 Wind yarn around each half of the pompom maker.

2 Put two the halves together to make a circle. Carefully, making sure you don't lose any ends, cut around the outside of the circle.

3 Tie a loose end of yarn tightly around the middle of the pompom. Try to wrap it around another time and tie a knot again to ensure the pompom is tied securely.

4 Pull the pompom maker apart to create the pompom.

5 Trim any straggly ends of yarn to make a neat ball.

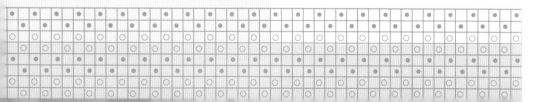

Tassels

Tassels are fun decorations for scarves and belts, and can be used to create plaits and fake hair.

2 Cut the bottom loop of the tassel and remove from cardboard carefully.

4 Pull the loop end a little way through the knitting.

1 Wind some yarn around a piece of card, cut to the length you want your tassel to be. This will ensure all your tassel's ends are the same length.

3 Push a crochet hook through the knitting, where you want the tassel to be. Grab the loop end of the tassel with the hook.

5 Tuck the cut ends through the loop.

6 Pull the cut ends tight.

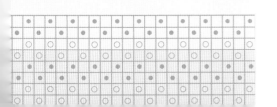

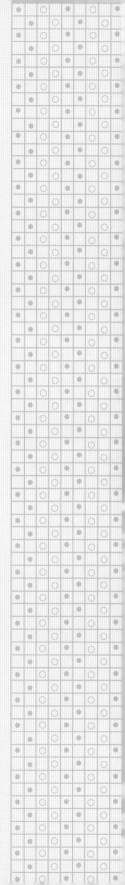

Warm and cozy knits

- 🐑 Cowl
- 🐑 Plait hat
- 🐑 Snake scarf
- 🐑 Earmuffs
- 🐑 Snowday earflap hat
- 🐑 Alpine adventures balaclava
- 🐑 Mouse mittens

Skill Level

Cowl

It is hard to believe, but this pattern is even easier than a scarf because it is not as long and so won't take as much time to knit!

MEASUREMENTS

❷ One size, approx 18in (46cm) all around and 7¼in (18cm) wide

SKILL LEVEL

❷ Easy

YARN

❷ 1 x 3½oz (100g)—approx 98yd (90m)—Rico Yarns Fashion Super Chunky, 60% new wool, 40% acrylic, in shade 13 teal

ALTERNATIVE YARNS

❷ Any super-bulky weight yarn,

although you could use the same principle to make a cowl out of any yarn—just knit a strip then sew it into a loop. The cowl will just come out thinner or thicker depending on the yarn!

GAUGE (TENSION)

❷ 11 sts and 18 rows to 4in (10cm) in garter stitch using US 13 (9mm) needles

NOTIONS

❷ Pair of US 13 (9mm) needles

❷ Darning needle

❷ Ribbon to decorate, if desired

Using US 13 (9mm) needles, cast on 20sts and work 18in (46cm), or desired length, in garter st (every row knit stitch).

Bind (cast) off all sts.

FINISHING

Sew two short sides together to form a tube.

Thread ribbon in and out through the cowl to decorate, if desired.

Wear either as it is or folded over to form a collar.

Skill Level

Plait Hat

This very basic pattern is a great project to practice shaping and you can knit it plain or striped without embellishment. Add the plaits or spiky hair for a fun hat or for your dressing-up box.

MEASUREMENTS

❶ S, M, L, to fit head up to 18(20:22)in (46(51:56)cm)

SKILL LEVEL

❶ Intermediate

YARN

❶ **Yarn A:** 1(2:2) x 1¾oz (50g)—approx 180yd (165m)—Rico : Baby Classic Aran, 50% acrylic, 50% polyamide, in shade 9755 pink

❶ **Yarn B:** 1 x 1¾oz (50g)—approx 137yd (125m)—Millamia Merino, 100% merino, in shade 142 daisy yellow

ALTERNATIVE YARNS

❶ Any worsted/Aran weight yarn is fine for this hat, but you can use whatever different yarns you wish for the hair—try textured yarns for curly hair, or bright colors for punk-style hair!

GAUGE (TENSION)

❶ 18 sts and 24 rows to 4in (10cm) in stockinette (stocking) stitch using US 8 (5mm) needles

NOTIONS

❶ Pair each of US 7 (4.5mm) and US 8 (5mm) needles
❶ Darning needle
❶ Cardboard to make plaits

Using US 7 (4.5mm) needles and yarn A, cast on 82(90:98) sts.

Row 1: k2, [p2, k2] to end of row.

Row 2: p2, [k2, p2] to end of row.

Repeat last two rows twice more. (Six rows worked.)

Change to larger needles and continue as folls:

Row 7: knit.

Row 8: purl.

Continue in stockinette (stocking) stitch as rows 7 and 8 until hat measures 5½(6:6)in (14(15:15)cm) from cast-on edge.

Decrease for Crown

Row 1: [k4, k2tog] to last 4(0:2) stitches, k4(0:2). (69(75:82) sts)

Row 2: purl.

Row 3: knit.

Row 4: purl.

Row 5: [k3, k2tog] to last 4(0:2) stitches, k4(0:2). (56(60:66) sts)

Row 6: purl.

Row 7: [k2, k2tog] to last 4(0:2) stitches, k4(0:2). (43(45:50) sts)

Row 8: purl.

Row 9: [k1, k2tog] to last 4(0:2) stitches, k4(0:2). (30(30:34) sts)

Row 10: purl.

Row 11: [k2tog] to end of row. (15(15:17) sts)

Row 12: purl.

Do not bind (cast) off, but cut yarn, leaving a long tail. Using a darning needle, thread tail through remaining 15[15:17] sts and pull up tight to gather into a circle. Sew up side seam using mattress stitch. Weave in all ends.

PLAITS

Cut a piece of cardboard to 16in (40cm) long. Wrap yarn B around cardboard 12 times, starting at bottom. Cut loops at bottom of cardboard and take off yarn, folded in half. Insert a length of yarn through loop at top and tie in place to hold yarn together. Ask a friend to hold the top loop while you plait. Split the 24 ends of yarn into 3 equal sections and plait the length, tying a knot in the bottom to secure.

Make another plait in the same way.

FINISHING

Sew one plait on either side of hat, to the inside of rib, with seam at the back.

Skill Level

Snake Scarf

Knitting a scarf can be boring, but this pattern certainly isn't! Use the basic scarf pattern with a head at one end and a tail at the other to create your own animal using felt, buttons, and fabric.

MEASUREMENTS

❶ One size—you can customize the length to fit you, but the scarf is approx 5in (12.5cm) wide

SKILL LEVEL

❶ Intermediate

YARN

❶ 1¾oz (50g)—approx 294yd (270m)—Debbie Bliss Cashmerino Aran, 55% merino wool, 33% microfiber, 12% cashmere, in:

Snake

❶ **Yarn A:** 2 x shade 502 lime

❶ **Yarn B:** 1 x shade 034 yellow

Cat

❶ **Yarn A:** 2 x shade 003 orange

❶ **Yarn B:** 1 x shade 009 gray

ALTERNATIVE YARNS

❶ Any Aran/worsted weight yarn will do, but you can use different thickness yarns and change your needles to match, the scarf will just come out bigger or smaller!

GAUGE (TENSION)

❶ Not essential, but 18 sts and 24 rows to 4in (10cm) in seed (moss) stitch using US 7 (4.5mm) needles is good

NOTIONS

❶ Pair of US 7 (4.5mm) needles

❶ Buttons for eyes

❶ Felt for tongue and ears or other features

❶ Darning needle

❶ Sewing needle and thread

Using US 7 (4.5mm) needles and yarn A, cast on 3 sts.

Row 1: k1, p1, k1.

Row 2: inc1, p1, inc1. (5 sts)

Row 3: p1, [k1, p1] to end of row.

Row 4: inc1, k1, p1, k1, inc1. (7 sts)

Row 5: k1, [p1, k1] to end of row. Seed (moss) pattern is set.

Row 6: inc1, p1, work seed (moss) st to last st, inc1. (9 sts)

Row 7: p1, [k1, p1] to end of row.

Row 8: inc1, k1, work seed (moss) st to last st, inc1. (11 sts)

Row 9: k1, [p1, k1] to end of row.

Row 10: inc1, p1, work seed (moss) st to last st, inc1. (13 sts)

Row 11: p1, [k1, p1] to end of row.

Row 12: inc1, k1, work seed (moss) st to last st, inc1. (15 sts)

Row 13: k1, [p1, k1] to end of row.

Row 14: inc1, p1, work seed (moss) st to last st, inc1. (17 sts)

Row 15: p1, [k1, p1] to end of row.

Row 16: inc1, k1, work seed (moss) st to last st, inc1. (19 sts)

Row 17: k1, [p1, k1] to end of row.

Row 18: inc1, p1, work seed (moss) st to last st, inc1. (21 sts)

Row 19: p1, [k1, p1] to end of row.

Row 20: inc1, k1, work seed (moss) st to last st, inc1. (23 sts)

Row 21: k1, [p1, k1] to end of row.

Repeat row 21 for 2¼in (6cm).

Change to yarn B and work 2¼in (6cm) as row 21.

Change to yarn A and work 2¼in (6cm) as row 21.

Continue working as row 21, changing color every 2¼in (6cm) until scarf measures approximately 1yd (1m), ending with a yarn B stripe.

Change to yarn A and work 4 rows in pattern.

Shape Head

Row 1: increase one stitch at either end of row, keeping to seed (moss) stitch as established. (25 sts)

Row 2: work straight in seed (moss) stitch.

Repeat last two rows until you have 31 sts.

Work straight in seed (moss) stitch pattern for 15 rows.

Next row: k2tog, work in seed (moss) stitch to last two sts, k2tog. (29 sts)

Next row: work straight in seed (moss) stitch.

Repeat last two rows until you have 17 sts.

Bind (cast) off all stitches.

FINISHING

Attach buttons to head for eyes.

Cut out a piece of felt into a forked tongue shape and sew to bottom of head for snake.

For cat, cut out some felt ears and a felt tongue and sew these to head. Stitch on a nose and mouth and add whiskers if you wish!

Skill Level

Earmuffs

If you don't like hats but can't stand having cold ears, earmuffs are for you— and they are great for when your friends just talk too loudly!

MEASUREMENTS

❂ One size, approx18in (46cm) from bottom of one ear to bottom of other

SKILL LEVEL

❂ Easy

YARN

❂ 1 x 1¾oz (50g)—approx 98yd (90m)—of Patons Fairytale Dreamtime DK, 100% pure wool, in each of:

❂ **Yarn A**: shade 4953 pink

❂ **Yarn B**: shade 4954 lilac

❂ **Yarn C**: shade 4957 turquoise

❂ **Yarn D**: shade 4952 lime

❂ **Yarn E**: shade 4960 yellow

ALTERNATIVE YARNS

❂ Any DK or sportweight yarn will do to achieve the same size earmuffs; choose something very warm, soft and cozy!

GAUGE (TENSION)

❂ 22 sts and 30 rows to 4in (10cm) in stockinette (stocking) stitch using US 6 (4mm) needles

NOTIONS

❂ Pair of US 6 (4mm) needles

❂ Darning needle

❂ Toy stuffing

Using US 6 (4mm) needles and yarn A, cast on 63 sts.

Row 1: purl.

Change to yarn B.

Row 2: [k7, k2tog] to end of row. (56 sts)

Row 3 (and every alt row): purl.

Row 4: [k6, k2tog] to end of row. (49 sts)

After the next purl row, change to yarn C.

Row 6: [k5, k2tog] to end of row. (42 sts)

Row 8: [k4, k2tog] to end of row. (35 sts)

After the next purl row, change to yarn D.

Row 10: [k3, k2tog] to end of row. (28 sts)

Row 12: [k2, k2tog] to end of row. (21 sts)

After the next purl row, change to yarn E.

Row 14: [k1, k2tog] to end of row. (14 sts)

Row 16: [k2tog] to end of row. (7 sts)

Thread yarn through remaining sts and pull up to form circle, sew up side seam.

Make one further piece in this way, then two further pieces entirely in yarn E, for the back of earmuff, without striping.

Sew one striped circle to one plain circle—so that both right sides face outward—all around circumference, leaving a small gap for stuffing. Fill with toy stuffing to desired fullness and sew up gap.

Do the same with two remaining circles.

BAND

Using US 6 (4mm) needles and yarn A cast on 12 sts and work in garter st, in two row stripes alternately of yarns A, B, C, D, and E until band measures 10in (25cm).

Bind (cast) off.

TIES

Finger-knit two lengths of chain approx 19¾in (50cm) long.

To finger-knit, make a slip knot and place it on your pointy/forefinger. Wrap another loop of yarn around your finger, closer to the end of the finger. Pull the slip knot over the second loop and off your finger, without dropping second loop—like binding (casting) off. Wrap another loop of yarn around your finger, closer to the end. Pull first loop over second loop and off your finger, without dropping second loop. Repeat for entire length of finger-knitting.

FINISHING

Sew an earmuff to either end of the band, with all right sides facing out.

Attach a tie to bottom of either earmuff to fasten under chin with a bow.

Skill Level

Snowday Earflap Hat

A multicolored hat to cheer you up and keep you warm on cold and dreary days. This yarn changes color as you knit, giving you the illusion of stripes without you having to change yarns—easy!

MEASUREMENTS

- L is up to 19¾in (50cm) head
M is up to 21¼in (54cm) head

SKILL LEVEL

- Intermediate

YARN

- 2(2) x 1¾oz (50g)—approx 190yd (174m)—Crystal Palace Yarns, Mochi Plus, 80% merino wool, 20% nylon, in shade 551 intense rainbow

ALTERNTIVE YARNS

- Any Aran weight yarn will do, you can stripe up a few different shades if you cannot find a variegated yarn that stripes itself. Wool or a wool mix yarn is great here for warmth

GAUGE (TENSION)

- 18 sts and 24 rows to 4in (10cm) in stockinette (stocking) stitch using US 8 (5mm) needles

NOTIONS

- Pair of US 8 (5mm) needles
- Stitch holders
- Darning needle

EARFLAPS (MAKE TWO)

Using US 8 (5mm) needles, cast on 6 sts.

Row 1(WS): purl.

Row 2: inc1, k to last st, inc1.

Repeat last two rows until there are 18 sts.

Next row: purl.

Leave each earflap on a stitch holder.

HAT

Using US 8 (5mm) needles, cast on 12(14) sts, knit across 18 sts from first earflap with right side facing, cast on 32(36), knit across 18 sts from second earflap with right side facing, cast on 12(14) sts. (92(100) sts)

Row 1(WS): purl across all sts.

Row 2: knit.

Continue in st st in this way on these 92(100) sts until work measures 4¾in (12cm) (5½in (14cm)) from cast-on brim, ending with a purl row.

Decrease for Crown

Row 1: [k4, k2tog] to last 2(4) sts, k2(4). (77(84) sts)

Beginning with a p row, work 3 rows st st.

Row 5: [k3, k2tog] to last 2(4) sts, k2(4). (62(68) sts)

Beginning with a p row, work 3 rows st st.

Row 9: [k2, k2tog] to last 2(4) sts, k2(4). (47(52) sts)

Row 10 (and every other row): purl.

Row 11: [k1, k2tog] to last 2(4) sts, k2(4). (32(36) sts

Row 13: [k2tog] to end of row. (16(18) sts)

Work in st st on these sts for 1¼in (3cm).

K2tog to end of row. (8(9) sts)

Thread yarn through remaining sts, pull up tight.

FINISHING

Rejoin yarn to one end of lower edge. With right side facing, pick up and knit 107[115] sts all along edge.

Row 1(WS): [k1, p1] to last st, k1.

Row 2: [p1, k1] to last st, p1.

Repeat rows 1–2 once more.

Bind (cast) off loosely in rib. Sew up side seam.

Skill Level

Alpine Adventures Balaclava

A great pattern for keeping your ears, head, and neck warm.

MEASUREMENTS
❶ To fit 6–8(9–10) yrs

SKILL LEVEL
❶ Difficult

YARN
❶ 2 x 1¾oz (50g)—approx 262yd (240m)—Rico Essentials Merino DK, 100% merino wool, in shade 39 petrol

ALTERNATIVE YARNS
❶ Any DK weight yarn will do, you can also stripe the balaclava or knit the ribbing in a different color for a different look

GAUGE (TENSION)
❶ 22 sts and 28 rows to 4in (10cm) in stockinette (stocking) stitch using US 6 (4mm) needles

NOTIONS
❶ Pair each of US 3 (3.25mm) and US 6 (4mm) needles
❶ Stitch holder
❶ Darning needle

Using US 6 (4mm) needles, cast on 73(83) sts.

Row 1(RS): k2, [p1, k1] to last st, k1.

Row 2: p2, [k1, p1] to last st, p1.

Repeat last two rows for ¾in (2cm), ending with a row 2.

Change to US 3 (3.25mm) needles and continue in rib as rows one and two until work measures 2¼(2¾)in (6(7)cm) ending with a row 2.

Next row: rib to last 9(11) sts. Turn. Leave these 9(11) sts on a stitch holder, unworked.

Next row: rib across to to last 9(11) sts. Turn. Leave these 9(11) sts on another stitch holder, unworked. (55(61) sts)

Next row: rib 3, *inc1, rib 6(5); repeat from * to last 3(4) sts, inc1, rib to end. (63(71) sts)

Next row: purl.

Change to US 6 (4mm) needles.

Row 1: knit.

Row 2: purl.

Continue in stockinette (stocking) stitch in this way until work measures 9(10¾)in (23(27)cm) from cast on edge, ending with a purl row.

Next row: bind (cast) off 21(24) sts, k to end.

Next row: bind (cast) off 21(24) sts, p to end.

Continue in stockinette (stocking) stitch on these remaining 21(23) sts until this center panel is as long as the edges just bound (cast) off.

Bind (cast) off all sts.

FINISHING

Sew sides of center panel into position along bound- (cast-) off edges.

Border

With right side facing and US 3 (3.25mm) needles, slip first 9(11) sts from stitch holder onto needle, rejoin yarn, pick up and knit 41(43) sts along side panel, 19(21) sts along center panel, 41(43) sts along other side panel, then rib across sts on second holder. (119(129) sts)

Starting with a row 2, work 7(9) rows of rib as for rows 1–2 of projct.

Bind (cast) off all sts in rib.

Sew up neck seam.

Skill Level

Mouse Mittens

These mittens will keep you warm and act as a toy at the same time. Have your own puppet show and make each hand a different animal!

MEASUREMENTS

- To fit 6-8(9-11) yrs

SKILL LEVEL

- Difficult

YARN

- 1(1) x 1¾oz (50g)—approx 131yd (120m)—Artesano Inca Cloud, 100% alpaca, in each of:
- **Yarn A**: shade ZK gray
- **Yarn B**: shade B432 pink

ALTERNATIVE YARNS

- Any DK or sportweight yarn will do. Try a warm and fluffy yarn and/or a mix of natural with man-made fibers for the warmth

and durability that mittens need. You can use all kinds of scraps of yarn for the embellishments, using different colors and textures for animals you may wish to create

GAUGE (TENSION)

- 24 sts and 32 rows to 4in (10cm) in stockinette (stocking) stitch using US 5 (3.75mm) needles

NOTIONS

- Pair each of US 3 (3.25mm) and US 5 (3.75mm) needles
- Darning needle
- Buttons for eyes

Using US 3 (3.25mm) needles and yarn A, cast on 41(45) sts.

Row 1(RS): k2, [p1, k1] to last st, k1.

Row 2: p2, [k1, p1] to last st, p1.

Repeat these two rows until rib measures 1½in (4cm), ending with a row 2.

Change to larger needles and st st and work 6(8) rows st st, beginning with a k row.

Increase for Thumb

Row 1: k19(21), inc into next st, k1, inc into next st, k to end. (43(47) sts)

Row 2 (and every even row): purl.

Row 3: k19(21), inc into next st, k3, inc into next st, k to end. (45(49) sts)

Row 5: k19(21), inc into next st, k5, inc into next st, k to end. (47(51) sts)

Continue to inc for thumb gusset in this way until you have 49(55) sts, ending with a k row.

Next row: purl.

Next row: k30(34), cast on 1 st, turn, leaving remaining sts unworked.

Next row: p12(14), cast on 1 st, turn and continue to work just on these 13(15) sts for 1½in (4cm), ending with a p row.

Shape Thumb Top

Next row: [k1, k2tog] to last 1(0) st, k1(0). (9(10) sts)

Next row: purl.

Next row: k1(0), [k2tog] to end. (5 sts)

Break off yarn and thread through remaining sts, pull up tightly and secure, sew up thumb seam.

Hand

With RS facing, rejoin yarn, pick up and knit 3 sts along base of thumb, knit remaining 19(21) unworked sts on left-hand needle.

Purl across all sts. (41(45) sts)

Work in st st for 2(2¼)in (5(6)cm) ending with a p row.

Shape Top

Row 1: [k1, k2tog, k15(17), k2tog] twice, k1. (37(41) sts)

Row 2 (and every even row): purl.

Row 3: [k1, k2tog, k13(15), k2tog] twice, k1. (33(37) sts)

Row 5: [k1, k2tog, k11(13), k2tog] twice, k1. (29(33) sts)

Row 7: [k1, k2tog, k9(11), k2tog] twice, k1. (25(29) sts)

Continue dec 4 sts every row as established until you have 17 sts.

Break off yarn and thread through remaining sts, pull up tightly and secure, sew up side seam.

OUTER EARS

Using US 5 (3.75mm) needles and yarn A, cast on 5 sts.

Row 1: knit.

Row 2: purl.

Row 3: inc1, k to last st, inc1. (7 sts)

Row 4: purl.

Row 5: inc1, k to last st, inc1. (9 sts)

Work three rows st st.

Row 9: k2tog, k to last 2 sts, k2tog. (7 sts)

Row 10: purl.

Row 11: k2tog, k to last 2 sts, k2tog. (5 sts)

Row 12: purl.

Bind (cast) off all sts.

Make three more pieces the same.

INNER EARS

Using US 5 (3.75mm) needles and yarn B, cast on 5 sts.

Rows 1–2: knit.

Row 3: inc1, k to last st, inc1. (7 sts)

Row 4: knit.

Row 5: inc1, k to last st, inc1. (9 sts)

Work four rows garter st (knit every row).

Row 10: ktog, k to last 2 sts, k2tog. (7 sts)

Row 11: knit.

Row 12: ktog, k to last 2 sts, k2tog. (5 sts)

Row 13: knit.

Bind (cast) off all sts.

Make three more pieces the same.

FINISHING

Sew each yarn A st st circle to a yarn B, garter st circle, with RS of st st piece on the outside.

Sew two ears to each mitten, to the top side.

Attach two small buttons for eyes to each mitten and embroider a nose and, if you wish, whiskers and other embellishments.

Accessories

- Pompom necklace
- Tassel belt
- Hair band
- Flowers
- Little bows
- Bling bracelets and necklace
- Decorative buttons
- Legwarmers
- School bag
- Fingerless mitts
- Pretty slippers

Skill Level

Pompom Necklace

Feel like a princess in this easy-to-make, fun-to-wear necklace. Use up your scraps of yarn from other projects to make the pompoms in whatever color mix you like. Here, the ends of balls from the zigzag cushion have been used to create the pompom beads. Make some French knitting bracelets to match!

MEASUREMENTS
- One size, approx 12in (30cm) drop

SKILL LEVEL
- Easy

YARN
- 1 x 1¾oz (50g)—approx 127yd (116m)—of Sublime Cashmere Merino Silk DK, 75% extra fine merino, 20% silk, 5% cashmere, in each of:
- **Yarn A**: shade 119 lido
- **Yarn B**: shade 124 splash
- **Yarn C**: shade 194 seesaw
- **Yarn D**: shade 195 puzzle
- **Yarn E**: shade 122 honeybunny

- **Yarn F**: shade 158 ladybug

ALTERNATIVE YARNS
- Use any yarn you wish for the necklace, using up scraps of yarn or mixing weights to create different-sized pompoms

GAUGE (TENSION)
- Not necessary

NOTIONS
- Pompom makers, various sizes, here they were ¾in (2cm) and 1in (2.5cm) in diameter
- French knitting bobbin
- Darning needle

NECKLACE

Make eight pompom beads (or the amount you wish) in varying sizes

Finger-knit (see page 41) a chain of approx 24in (61cm). Thread the pompom beads onto the chain, using the darning needle to thread the chain straight through the center of each pompom, then tie the chain into a circle.

BRACELETS

Using a French knitting bobbin according to the instructions on the pack make lengths of French knitting long enough to go around the widest part of your hand and sew into a loop.

You can make some pieces long enough for necklaces, too.

Skill Level

Tassel Belt

This is a perfect pattern for total beginners, using only the simplest knit stitch and some stripes to great effect. Make the belt and tassels as long as you wish.

MEASUREMENTS

- One size—you can customize the length to fit you, but the belt is approx 2¼in (6cm) wide

SKILL LEVEL

- Easy

YARN

- 1 x 1¾oz (50g)—approx 246yd (225m)—Debbie Bliss Eco Aran, 100% organic cotton, in each of:
- **Yarn A**: shade 620 lime

- **Yarn B**: shade 609 purple
- **Yarn C**: shade 621 jade

GAUGE (TENSION)

- 18 sts and 28 rows to 4in (10cm) in garter stitch using US 7 (4.5mm) needles

NOTIONS

- Pair of US 7 (4.5mm) needles
- A small crochet hook to pull through tassels
- Cardboard to make tassels
- Darning needle

Using US 7 (4.5mm) needles and yarn A, cast on 10 sts.

Row 1: knit.

Row 2: knit.

Change to yarn B.

Row 3: knit.

Row 4: knit.

Change to yarn C.

Row 5: knit.

Row 6: knit.

Change to yarn A.

Repeat these 6 rows, changing color every two rows until belt is desired length—enough to go round your waist and tie up—ending with two rows of yarn A.

Bind (cast) off all sts and weave in ends.

TASSELS

Cut a piece of cardboard to 4¾in (12cm) long (or desired length of tassel).

Wind yarn A round the cardboard five times, starting from the bottom of the card. Cut the loops at the bottom of the tassel and remove from card, still folded in half.

Insert crochet hook through the bottom right-hand corner of one end of belt and pull the looped end of tassel through for approx ½in (1cm). Pass the cut end of the tassel through the looped end and pull to secure. Repeat this twice more at even intervals along short end of belt, then repeat at opposite end.

Trim tassels to the same length.

Skill Level

Hair Band

A very easy, pretty and practical way of tidying your hair. Make lots of them to match your favorite outfits.

MEASUREMENTS

- To fit approx 19¾(20½:21¼)in (50(52:54)cm) head

SKILL LEVEL

- Easy

YARN

- 1 x 1¾oz (50g)—approx 127yd (115m)—of Twilleys Freedom Cotton DK, 100% organic cotton, in each of:
- **Yarn A:** 606 raspberry
- **Yarn B:** 605 wild rose

ALTERNATIVE YARNS

- Any DK weight yarn will be perfect for this project, and something that has a bit of elastic in may do even better!

GAUGE (TENSION)

- 22 sts and 28 rows to 4in (10cm) in stockinette (stocking) stitch using US 6 (4mm) needles

NOTIONS

- Pair of US 6 (4mm) needles
- Darning needle

Using US 6 (4mm) needles and yarn A, cast on 83(89:95) sts.

Row 1: k1, [p1, k1] to end of row.

Row 2: p1, [k1, p1] to end of row.

Change to yarn B and repeat last two rows.

Change to yarn A.

Repeat last 4 rows once more, then repeat rows 1–2 in yarn A.

Bind (cast) off all sts.

FINISHING

Sew two short ends together to form a loop. Sew in all ends.

Skill Level

Flowers

You only need basic knit stitch for this project, although you could knit flowers in whatever stitch you like. The yarn thickness does not matter, as the flowers will just be bigger or smaller depending on what you use. Pop flowers on hair grips, alice bands, brooch backs, and more, and embellish them with buttons and ribbons for versatile accessories.

MEASUREMENTS

❷ Small (large) sizes
These vary depending on yarn, needle size, and how tightly you roll them when making up, but they are approximately 2–3in (5–7.5cm) in diameter

SKILL LEVEL

❷ Easy

YARN

❷ Use any scraps of yarn left over from your other projects— these flowers do not take much yarn. You could also stripe them up with lots of short leftover lengths of yarn. We have used a variety of different Aran/worsted weight yarns from the other projects in the book.

GAUGE (TENSION)

❷ Not necessary

NOTIONS

❷ We used US 8 (5mm) needles to go with our Aran/worsted weight yarn, but you can use whichever needles the ball band of the yarn you are using asks for
❷ Buttons to decorate as desired
❷ Brooch back/hair grip/safety pin for fastening
❷ Darning needle
❷ Sewing needle and thread

Using US 8 (5mm) needles and Aran weight yarn, cast on 50(70) sts and knit every row (garter stitch) for 6–10 rows, until the flower is about half the diameter you want it, adding stripes of different colors if you wish.

Don't bind (cast) off, but cut your yarn, leaving enough to sew up, thread the tail through all stitches on needle, and pull up gently to gather the flower as much as you wish.

Curl the strip around on itself into a coil and secure with some stitches at the back to hold it in shape.

FINISHING

Decorate as desired with a button and/or ribbons, sewing buttons to the front and ribbons around the back.

Attach the sort of fastening you want at the back—for example, a safety pin or brooch back to make a brooch or corsage.

Skill Level

Little Bows

Bows to put in your hair or wear as brooches. The shiny yarn is very pretty and the pattern is so easy that you can even play with the stitch used to make bows with different textures

MEASUREMENTS

❂ One size, approx 2¾in (7cm) wide

SKILL LEVEL

❂ Easy

YARN

❂ 1 x 1¾oz (50g)—approx 127yd (116m)—Sublime Cashmere Merino Silk DK, 75% extra fine merino, 20% silk, 5% cashmere, in each of:

❂ **Yarn A:** shade 208 neroli
❂ **Yarn B:** shade 209 organdie
❂ **Yarn C:** shade 210 Thai tea
❂ **Yarn D:** shade 212 saffron
❂ **Yarn E:** shade 214 kimono

ALTERNATIVE YARNS

❂ Any DK weight yarn will do here, but you could try any yarn; bows will just come out different sizes. The yarn used here is silky, but you could try a matt yarn, or a mixture of shiny and matt for different textures

GAUGE (TENSION)

❂ 22 sts and 32 rows to 4in (10cm) in garter using US 6 (4mm) needles

NOTIONS

❂ Pair of US 6 (4mm) needles
❂ Darning needle
❂ Safety pins/brooch backs
❂ Hair grips/headbands
❂ Sewing needle and thread

Using US 6 (4mm) needles, cast on 10 sts and work in garter st (every row knit) for 5½in (14cm) or twice desired length for bow.

Bind (cast) off.

Sew short ends together to form a loop.

Using US 6 (4mm) needles, cast on 5 sts and work in st st (one row knit, one row purl) for 10 rows.

Bind (cast) off.

FINISHING

Wrap st st strip around middle of garter st loop and sew together short ends at back.

Sew a hairgrip, brooch back or safety pin to back of bow.

Make up the bows in different colors, or mix and match the colors of bow and tie sections, or even stripe the bows for differing styles.

Skill Level

Bling Bracelets and Necklace

When you get a little bored of your knitting, put it down and have a break to French knit this quick-and-easy jewellery, perfect for gifts, or just to wear yourself!

MEASUREMENTS

➊ One size

SKILL LEVEL

➋ Intermediate

YARN

➊ 1 x 1¾oz (50g)—approx 127yd (116m)—of Sublime Cashmere Merino Silk DK, 75% extra fine merino, 20% silk, 5% cashmere, in each of:

➊ **Yarn A:** shade 124 splash

➊ **Yarn B:** shade 194 seesaw

➊ **Yarn C:** shade 009 pink

➊ **Yarn D:** shade td53 purple

ALTERNATIVE YARNS

➊ Any DK or sportweight yarn will do, although you could use any weight of yarn and and change the size of the jewels to suit it

GAUGE (TENSION)

➊ Not necessary

NOTIONS

➊ French knitting bobbin

➊ Darning needle

➊ Assorted beads, sequins or buttons for added "bling"

➊ Sewing needle and thread

Following the instructions included with the bobbin, French knit a length of tube long enough to either wear around your wrist or to the desired length of necklace.

Fasten off the tube according to the instructions on the pack.

Sew the two ends of tube together to form a loop. Sew on desired beads and embellishments for the amount of "bling" you require.

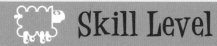

Skill Level

Decorative Buttons

Use up all your scraps making these bright and beautiful covered buttons that you can use on your clothes instead of your boring old buttons, or as badges on coats and bags.

MEASUREMENTS

❷ Buttons used are 1½in (38mm), 1¼in (29mm), 7/8in (23mm) and 5/8in (15mm)

SKILL LEVEL

❷ Easy

YARN

❷ Oddments of yarn from all the DK/worsted weight projects in the book

GAUGE (TENSION)

❷ Not essential but roughly 22 sts and 28 rows to 4in (10cm) in stockinette (stocking) stitch using US 6 (4mm) needles

NOTIONS

❷ Pair of US 6 (4mm) needles
❷ Darning needle
❷ Self-cover buttons kit

LARGE BUTTON

Using US 6 (4mm) needles and any yarn, cast on 11 sts and work in st st until piece is square, striping colors as desired.

Bind (cast) off all sts.

MEDIUM BUTTONS

Using US 6 (4mm) needles and any yarn, cast on 8 sts and work in st st until piece is square, striping colors as desired.

Bind (cast) off all sts.

SMALL BUTTONS

Using US 6 (4mm) needles and any yarn, cast on 5 sts and work in st st until piece is square, striping colors as desired.

Bind (cast) off all sts.

Cover all buttons with the squares of knitting, following the instructions on the kit.

Sew to garments or accessories as decoration, or in place of existing buttons.

Skill Level

Legwarmers

These legwarmers are great for keeping you warm in winter or for wearing to dance or gym classes.

MEASUREMENTS

❶ To fit approx 8¼(9:10)in (21(23:25)cm) calf; you can make the legwarmers as long or as short as you wish

SKILL LEVEL

❶ Easy

YARN

❶ 1 x 1¾oz (50g)—approx 196yd (180m)—Debbie Bliss Cashmerino Aran, 55% merino wool, 33% microfiber, 12% cashmere, in each of:
❶ **Yarn A**: shade 31 dark purple
❶ **Yarn B**: shade 17 light Purple

ALTERNATIVE YARNS

❶ Any worsted/Aran weight yarn is fine for these legwarmers

GAUGE (TENSION)

❶ 18 sts and 24 rows to 4in (10cm) in stockinette (stocking) stitch using US 8 (5mm) needles

NOTIONS

❶ Pair each of US 7 (4.5mm) and US 8 (5mm) needles
❶ Darning needle

Using US 7 (4.5mm) needles and yarn A, cast on 37(41:45) sts.

Row 1: k1, [p1, k1] to end of row.

Row 2: p1, [k1, p1] to end of row.

Repeat rib rows 1–2 until work measures 4in (10cm) from cast on, ending with a row 2.

Change to US 8 (5mm) needles and yarn B.

Next row: knit.

Next row: purl.

Continue in stockinette (stocking) stitch as last two rows until stockinette (stocking) stitch section measures 6in (15cm), or to desired leg length, ending with a purl row.

Change back to US 7 (4.5mm) needles and yarn A.

Next row: k1, [p1, k1] to end of row.

Next row: p1, [k1, p1] to end of row.

Repeat last two rib rows for a further 4in (10cm).

Bind (cast) off all sts.

FINISHING

Sew up long side seam of each legwarmer using whip stitch.

 **Skill Level**

School Bag

A handy bag to hold all your stationery for school, or your goodies on a day out.

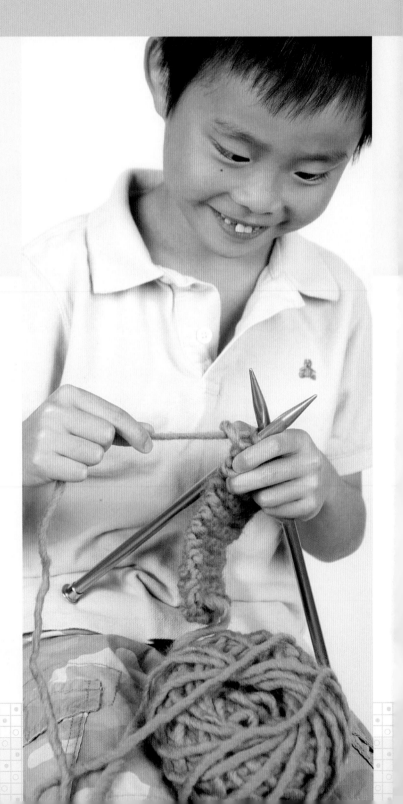

MEASUREMENTS

❷ One size, approx 12¼in wide by 8in deep (31cm wide by 20cm deep)

SKILL LEVEL

❷ Intermediate

YARN

❷ 1 x 3½oz (100g)—approx 196yd (180m)—Rico Fashion Super Chunky, 60% new wool, 40% acrylic, in each of:
❷ **Yarn A**: shade 04 navy
❷ **Yarn B**: shade 08 mustard

ALTERNATIVE YARNS

❷ Any super bulky weight yarn will work well

GAUGE (TENSION)

❷ 9 sts and 12 rows to 4in (10cm) in stockinette (stocking) stitch using US 15 (10mm) needles

NOTIONS

❷ Pair of US 15 (10mm) needles
❷ Darning needle
❷ Sewing needle and thread
❷ Fabric measuring 17¾ x 12in (45 x 30cm)
❷ Snap fastener
❷ Ribbon, if desired

Using US 15 (10mm) needles and yarn A, cast on 30 sts.

Row 1 (RS): knit.

Row 2: purl.

Continue in st st in this way until 17¾in (45cm) has been worked ending with a k row.

Change to yarn B and work 4 rows garter st (every row knit).

Bind (cast) off all sts.

STRAP

Using US 15 (10mm) needles and yarn B, cast on 5 sts and work approx 1yd (1m) in garter st (every row knit) or until desired strap length is worked.

Bind (cast) off all sts.

FINISHING

Turning under a narrow hem, slip stitch fabric to wrong side of bag piece, ensuring there is at least a ½in (1cm) gap to edge of knitting all around.

Fold over piece from bottom, to create an 8in (20cm) deep pouch. Sew up side seams.

Fold over top flap (with contrast stripe) and sew a snap fastener to the center of this flap on the wrong side, with corresponding part on right side of pouch.

Sew short ends of strap to either side of bag, along top of pouch.

Thread ribbon through stitches above stripe on flap if desired and tie into a bow.

 **Skill Level**

Fingerless Mitts

Lots of people think knitting gloves is hard, but these mitts are just straight rectangles sewn up the side, so there is no excuse for not making them! Knit them as long or short as you wish, depending on how warm you want your arms to be.

MEASUREMENTS
- S(M:L) to fit approx 6¾(7½:8¼)in (17(19:21)cm) wrist

SKILL LEVEL
- Easy

YARN
- 1 x 1¾oz (50g)—approx 131yd (120m)—Rico Essentials Merino DK, 100% merino wool, in each of:

Long gloves:
- Yarn A: shade 04 acacia
- Yarn B: shade 73 orange
- Yarn C: shade 66 sun

Short gloves:
- Yarn A: shade 38 dark blue
- Yarn B: shade 23 light blue
- Yarn C: shade 18 bright blue

ALTERNATIVE YARNS
- Any DK weight yarn, you could use self-striping yarn if you can't be bothered to stripe different colors, or even do them in one color. A yarn which has some man-made fiber content— such as nylon or acrylic— would be good, as these mitts will see a lot of wear and the man-made fiber will make them more durable

GAUGE (TENSION)
- 22 sts and 28 rows to 4in (10cm) in seed (moss) stitch using US 6 (4mm) needles

NOTIONS
- Pair each of US 5 (3.75mm) and US 6 (4mm) needles
Darning needle

Using US 5 (3.75mm) needles and yarn A, cast on 37(41:45) sts.

Row 1: k1, [p1, k1] to end of row.

Row 2: p1, [k1, p1] to end of row.

Repeat last two rows for 1in (2.5cm) for short gloves, or 4¼in (11cm) for long gloves, or for desired length, ending with a row 2.

Change to US 6 (4mm) needles and yarn B.

Row 1: knit.

Row 2: purl.

Change to yarn C.

Row 3: knit.

Row 4: purl.

Change to yarn A.

Row 5: knit.

Row 6: purl.

Continue in stockinette (stocking) stitch (one row knit, one row purl) as for rows 1–6, changing color every two rows until striped section measures 2½(2¾:3¼)in (6(7:8)cm), ending with a purl row.

Change to US 5 (3.75mm) needles and yarn A.

Row 1: k1, [p1, k1] to end of row.
Row 2: p1, [k1, p1] to end of row.
Repeat these two rows once more.
Bind (cast) off all sts.

FINSHING

All lengths: sew up side seam on each glove from bottom of long rib to ½in (1cm) from beginning of striped section. Leave a gap of 1½in (4cm), and then sew up rest of seam to top of shorter rib.

Pretty Slippers

Slippers don't have to be boring, try these out for size! Customize them to make ballet slippers, ruby slippers, or even football boots.

MEASUREMENTS

- S[M:L] to fit foot approx 7(7¾:8¼)in (17.5(19.5:21)cm) long

SKILL LEVEL

- Intermediate

YARN

Ballet slippers

- 2(2:2) x 1¾oz (50g)—approx 127yd (116m)—of Sublime Cashmere Merino Silk DK, 75% extra fine merino, 20% silk, 5% cashmere, in shade 009 pink

Ruby slippers

- 2(2:2) x 1¾oz (50g)—approx 127yd (116m)—of Sublime Cashmere Merino Silk DK, 75% extra fine merino, 20% silk, 5% cashmere, in shade 192 teddy bear

ALTERNATIVE YARNS

- Any DK or sportweight yarn will do to achieve the same size slippers. It is best to use a yarn with at least a little man-made fiber in for durability. You could try some sock yarns.

GAUGE (TENSION)

- 22 sts and 28 rows to 4in (10cm) in stockinette (stocking) stitch using US 6 (4mm) needles

NOTIONS

- Pair of US 6 (4mm) needles
- Darning needle
- Ribbons
- Buttons

Basic Slipper Pattern

Using US 6 (4mm) needles cast on 22(25:28) sts.

Work in garter st (every row knit), increasing 1 st at either end of every alt row until there are 38(41:44) sts.

Work two rows straight.

Continue in garter st, decreasing 1 st at either end of every alt row until you are back to 22(25:28) sts.

Cast on 8(10:10) sts at beginning of next row for heel. (30(35:38) sts)

Continue in garter st, keeping heel edge straight and increasing 1 st at toe edge every alt row until there are 38(43:46) sts, ending at heel edge.

Bind (cast) off 20(25:28) sts, k to end. (18 sts)

Knit 13(15:15) further rows on remaining 18 sts, cast on 20(25:28) sts at end of last row. (38(43:46) sts)

Keeping heel straight, work on these sts, decreasing 1 st at toe edge on every alt row until 30(35:38) sts remain.

Bind (cast) off all sts.

Join heel seam and edges around sole, working in all fullness at toe.

Ruby slippers

STRAP (MAKE TWO)

Cast on 5 sts and work 4¼in (11cm) in garter st.

Next row: k2, yo, k2tog, k1.

Work in garter st until strap measures 4¾in (12cm).

Bind (cast) off all stitches.

Attach one strap to right inner ankle edge on first slipper and one to left inner ankle edge on second slipper.

Attach buttons to opposite sides top edge to align with buttonholes in straps.

Ballet Slippers.

HEEL TAB (MAKE TWO)

Cast on 8 sts and work 2½in (6cm) in garter st.

Bind (cast) off all sts.

Sew each tab into a loop at the top of heel. Thread a ribbon through each loop to tie around ankles.

Bedroom essentials

- Hot-water bottle cover
- Change purse
- MP3/phone cover
- Patchwork blanket
- Caterpillar doorstop
- Heart cushion
- Ladybug lavender bags
- Rainbow pillow cover

Skill Level

Hot-Water Bottle Cover

A simple rectangle can be made into a cute and cozy hot-water bottle cover that would make a pretty gift.

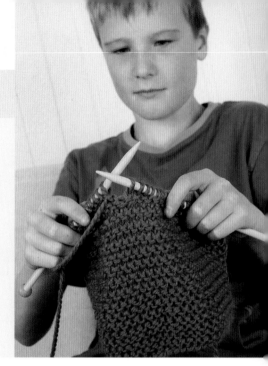

MEASUREMENTS

❶ One size, to fit an average hot-water bottle cover, approx 9in wide x 14in high (23cm wide x 36cm high)

SKILL LEVEL

❷ Easy

YARN

❸ 1 x 3½oz (100g)—approx 218yd (200m)—BC Garn Manu, 100% baby alpaca, in each of:
❹ **Yarn A:** shade un23 light teal
❺ **Yarn B:** shade un05 dark teal

ALTERNATIVE YARNS

❶ Any bulky weight yarn will do for this project. Try to find a soft and cozy yarn that you will enjoy cuddling and that will keep your bottle hot as long as possible

GAUGE (TENSION)

❷ 13 sts and 15 rows to 4in (10cm) in stockinette (stocking) stitch using US 11 (8mm) needles

NOTIONS

❸ Pair of US 11 (8 mm) needles
❹ Darning needle
❺ Approx 1yd (1m) of ½in (1cm) wide ribbon
❻ Hot-water bottle

Using US 11 (8mm) needles and yarn A, cast on 60 sts.

Work 3in (7.5cm) in garter st (every row knit).

Change to yarn B.

Next row: purl.

Next row: knit.

Continue in stockinette (stocking) stitch for 3in (7.5cm), ending with a purl row.

Change back to yarn A.

Work 8in (20cm) in garter st (every row knit).

Bind (cast) off all sts.

FINISHING

Fold rectangle in half widthways and sew up the bottom and side seam.

Thread ribbon in and out of the stitches all around, approx 2½in (6.5cm) down from opening.

Slip hot water bottle into the pouch made, pull up the ribbon and tie in a bow.

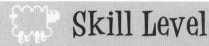

Skill Level

Change Purse

Keep all your loose change in this sweet purse and hide it away so your little brother or sister doesn't find it! Or use the purse to store favorite hair accessories and other treasures.

MEASUREMENTS

❷ One size, approx 4in (10cm) wide by 4in (10cm) tall

SKILL LEVEL

❷ Easy

YARN

❷ 1 x 1¾oz (50g)—approx 127yd (116m)—of Sublime Cashmere Merino Silk DK, 75% extra fine merino, 20% silk, 5% cashmere, in each of:

❷ **Yarn A**: shade 127 chicory

❷ **Yarn B**: shade 050 dilly

❷ **Yarn C**: shade 162 pinkaboo

ALTERNATIVE YARNS

❷ Any DK or sportweight yarn will achieve the same size purse, although you could use any weight of yarn and the purse will simply come out a different size

GAUGE (TENSION)

❷ 22 sts and 28 rows to 4in (10cm) in stockinette (stocking) stitch using US 6 (4mm) needles

NOTIONS

❷ Pair of US 6 (4mm) needles

❷ Darning needle

❷ Snap fastener

❷ Fabric 4 x 10in (10 x 23cm)

❷ Sewing needle and thread

Using US 6 (4mm) needles, and yarn A, cast on 25 sts.

Row 1(RS): k1, [p1, k1] to end of row.

Repeat last row five times more.

Change to yarn B, do not fasten off yarn A.

Next row: knit.

Change to yarn C, do not fasten off yarn B.

Next row: purl.

Continue in st st until work measures 9¼in (23.5cm), striping in one row stripes of yarns A, B, and C alternately, ending with a yarn C row.

Change to yarn A.

Next row: k1, [p1, k1] to end of row.

Repeat last row five times more.
Bind (cast) off all sts.

FINISHING

Turning under a narrow hem, slip stitch fabric to wrong side of knitted strip between seed (moss) stitch borders, leaving a gap of ¼in (0.5cm) at knitting edges for sewing up purse.

Fold strip up from bottom to create pouch approx 4in (10cm) deep and sew up side seam.

Attach a snap fastener to flap and main body of purse to close.

Skill Level

MP3/Phone Cover

A practical way to store your MP3 player or phone so that it doesn't get knocked around as you travel.

MEASUREMENTS

❷ One size, approx 4¾in (12cm) long by 2in (5cm) wide: will stretch to approx 2¾in (7cm) wide

SKILL LEVEL

❷ Easy

YARN

❷ 1 x 1¾oz (50g)—approx 137yd (125m)—Millamia Merino, 100% merino, in each of:

❷ **Yarn A**: shade 161 seaside

❷ **Yarn B**: shade 120 forget-me-not

ALTERNATIVE YARNS

❷ Any DK or sportweight yarn will make a cover about the same size as this one

GAUGE (TENSION)

❷ 30 sts and 30 rows to 4in (10cm) in 1 x 1 rib using US 3 (3.25mm) needles

NOTIONS

❷ Pair of US 3 (3.25mm) needles

❷ Darning needle

❷ Button approx ¾in (2cm) in diameter

Using US 3 (3.25mm) needles and yarn A, cast on 31 sts and work in rib as folls:

Row 1(RS): k2, [p1, k1] to last st, k1.

Row 2: p2, [k1, p1] to last st, p1.

Change to yarn B and work 2 rows in rib, as rows 1–2.

Work 4¾in (12cm) in rib, alternating in stripes of yarn A and B, ending with a row 1.

Next row: bind (cast) off 16 sts, rib to end of row. (15 sts)

Work on these 15 sts for 1½in (4cm), ending with a row 2.

Bind (cast) off all sts.

FINISHING

Fold piece widthways, with flap at top. Sew up bottom and side seams.

Work 2¼in (6cm) of finger-knitting (see page 41) and attach it to center of flap in a loop.

Attach button to main body of cover, corresponding to finger-knitted loop.

Skill Level

Patchwork Blanket

A patchwork blanket made of squares is the perfect way to try out new stitches—just knit a different stitch in every swatch and sew them all together. It's easier to sew up if all the squares are the same size, but you can make them different sizes for a mismatched look.

MEASUREMENTS

❶ One size, each square approx 12 x 12in (30 x 30cm)

SKILL LEVEL

❶ Easy

YARN

❶ 1 x 3½oz (100g) BC Garn Tundra, 100% merino wool, in each of:

❶ **Yarn A**: shade td00 cream

❶ **Yarn B**: shade td02 light blue

❶ **Yarn C**: shade td06 pink

❶ **Yarn D**: shade td13 beige

❶ **Yarn E**: shade td16 yellow

❶ **Yarn F**: shade td18 green

❶ **Yarn G**: shade td53 purple

ALTERNATIVE YARNS

❶ Any bulky or super bulky yarn can be substituted, but if you just want to use up scraps of yarn to make a blanket, that is fine, too. Because a specific gauge (tension) is not necessary, you can just make the blanket whichever size you wish.

GAUGE (TENSION)

❶ 10 sts and 15 rows to 4in (10cm) in stockinette (stocking) stitch using US 13 (9mm) needles

NOTIONS

❶ Pair of US 13 (9mm) needles

❶ Darning needle

SQUARE ONE

Using US 13 (9mm) needles and any yarn you wish, cast on 30 sts.

Work 12in (30cm) in garter st (every row knit).

Bind (cast) off all sts.

SQUARE TWO

Using US 13 (9mm) needles and any yarn you wish, cast on 30 sts.

Work 12in (30cm) in stockinette (stocking) st (one row knit, one row purl).

Bind (cast) off all sts.

Make six of each square, in a mixture of colors, adding stripes if you wish.

FINISHING

To sew up the squares, lay them all out flat and arrange as you like, with three squares wide and four squares long. Try to attach them with one side edge to one cast-on or bound-(cast-) off edge as this will help to neaten the squares.

Using a contrast color of your choice—either a left-over bit of yarn from the squares or any other yarn or thread—sew up the squares using whip stitch.

Fasten off all ends and steam very lightly into shape.

Skill Level

Caterpillar Doorstop

Use this cute caterpillar as a doorstop or draught excluder.

MEASUREMENTS

❶ One size, approx 26½in (67cm) long

SKILL LEVEL

❷ Intermediate

YARN

❸ 1 x 1¾oz (50g)—approx 87yd (80m)—Debbie Bliss Rialto Aran, 100% merino, in each of:
❶ **Yarn A:** shade 22 pale green
❶ **Yarn B:** shade 10 green
❶ **Yarn C:** shade 23 baby blue
❶ **Yarn D:** shade 08 purple

ALTERNATIVE YARNS

❶ Any Aran/worsted weight yarn will be work well; you could even use up old scraps of yarn and make a multicolored, stripy version

GAUGE (TENSION)

❶ 18 sts and 24 rows to 4in (10cm) in stockinette (stocking) stitch using US 8 (5mm) needles

NOTIONS

❶ Pair of US 8 (5mm) needles
❶ Darning needle
❶ Toy stuffing
❶ Pompom maker
❶ Buttons for eyes

BODY

Using US 8 (5mm) needles, and yarn A, cast on 5 sts.
Row 1 (and every other row): purl.
Row 2: knit twice into each st to end of row. (10 sts)
Row 4: knit twice into each st to end of row. (20 sts)
Row 6: [k1, inc1] to end of row. (30 sts)
Row 8: [k2, inc1] to end of row. (40 sts)
Row 10: [k3, inc1] to end of row. (50 sts)

Work ¾in (2cm) straight in yarn A.

Change to yarn B and work ¾in (2cm) straight.

Change to yarn C and work ¾in (2cm) straight.

Continue in st st in alternating ¾in (2cm) stripes of three colors until piece measures approx 25in (63.5cm), ending with a p row and a complete stripe.

Continue in color of next stripe only.
Next row: [k3, k2tog] to end of row. (40 sts)
Next row (and every other row): purl.
Next row: [k2, k2tog] to end of row. (30 sts)
Next row: [k1, k2tog] to end of row. (20 sts)

Next row: [k2tog] to end of row. (10 sts)

Next row: [k2tog] to end of row. (5 sts)

Do not bind (cast) off, but thread through remaining sts, pull up tight and secure in circle. Sew up side seam, leaving a gap to stuff. Stuff tube then sew up gap.

Thread yarn in and out all round tube approx 4in (10cm) down from one end, pull up to make head and secure. Repeat at other end for tail.

LEGS (MAKE EIGHT, OR MORE!!)

Using US 8 (5mm) needles and yarn D, cast on 8 sts.

Work ¾in (2cm) in garter st.

Bind (cast) off 4 sts, work straight in garter st on these 4 sts for a further ¾in (2cm).

Bind (cast) off all sts.

FINISHING

Attach legs along body, divided and spaced evenly on both sides between head and tail.

Make two pompoms and attach to head for antennae. Sew on two buttons for eyes, and embroider nose and smile in yarn D.

Skill Level

Heart Cushion

Who needs a boring old square cushion when you can decorate your bed with heart-shaped ones? These are also perfect gifts for moms on Mother's Day or Valentine's Day. You can vary how you stuff these cushions, making them sweet-smelling, lavender-filled sachets, mini beanbags, or squishy, soft pillows.

MEASUREMENTS

❂ One size, approx 7¼in (18cm) at widest point and 6¼in (16cm) tall

SKILL LEVEL

❂ Intermediate

YARN

❂ 1 x 1¾oz (50g)—approx 127yd (116m)—of Sublime Cashmere Merino Silk DK, 75% extra fine merino, 20% silk, 5% cashmere, in each of:

❂ **Yarn A:** shade 159 pansy

❂ **Yarn B:** shade 162 pinkaboo

ALTERNATIVE YARNS

❂ Any DK or sportweight yarn will do to achieve the same size cushion, although you could use any weight of yarn and the cushion will simply come out a different size

GAUGE (TENSION)

❂ 22 sts and 28 rows to 4in (10cm) in stockinette (stocking) stitch using US 6 (4mm) needles

NOTIONS

❂ Pair of US 6 (4mm) needles

❂ Stitch holder

❂ Darning needle

❂ Toy stuffing, beanbag beans, or dried lavender

Using US 6 (4mm) needles and yarn A, cast on 5 sts.

Row 1: knit.

Row 2: inc1, k to last st, inc1. (7 sts)

Change to yarn B.

Repeat these two rows until you have 17 sts, changing color evey two rows and ending with a row 2.

Break off these yarns and leave these 17 sts in holder.

Make one more piece the same, but do not break off yarns on second piece. Continue in two-row stripe pattern, turn and work across 17 sts of this piece, cast on one stitch, then knit across 17 sts on stitch holder. (35 sts)

Knit one row.

Next row: inc1, k to last st, inc1. (37 sts)

Next row: knit one row.

Work last two rows once more, then work in garter stitch for eight rows. (39 sts)

Next row: k2tog, k to last 2 sts, k2tog. (37 sts)

Work 3 rows garter st.

Repeat last 4 rows twice more.
(33 sts)

Next row: k2tog, k to last 2sts,
k2tog. (31 sts)

Next row: knit one row.

Repeat last two rows until
3 sts remain.

Next row: k3tog.

Fasten off yarn.

Make one more piece for the back
using yarn A only.

FINISHING

Sew together two pieces, leaving
small gap in seam for stuffing. Fill
with toy stuffing or chosen filling
to desired fullness. Sew up gap.

Skill Level

Ladybug Lavender Bags

These sweet lavender bags are so cute you may not want to pop them away in your drawers or wardrobe, but leave them near a radiator to freshen the room naturally. You may even wish to stuff them instead with toy stuffing to create a regular toy, or with beanbag granules to make beanbag bugs.

MEASUREMENTS

❷ **Large bug:** approx 4in (10cm) wide

❷ **Small bug:** approx 2½in (6.5cm) wide

SKILL LEVEL

❷ Intermediate

YARN

❷ **Yarn A:** 1 x 1¾oz (50g)—approx 137yd (125m)—Millamia Merino, 100% merino,

Large bug: shade 140 scarlet

Small bug: shade 143 fuchsia

❷ **Yarn B:** 1 x 1¾oz (50g)—approx 131yd (120m)—Rico Essentials Merino DK, 100% merino wool, in shade 90, black

ALTERNATIVE YARNS

❷ This project uses only small amounts of yarn, so you could use scraps of any other DK or sportweight yarn to create the ladybugs

GAUGE (TENSION)

❷ This is not essential but 23 sts to 4in (10cm) in garter stitch using US 5 (3.75mm) needles is good to aim for

NOTIONS

❷ Pair of US 5 (3.75mm) needle

❷ Assorted buttons for eyes and spots

❷ Each bug needs two small circles of fabric to make pouch for the filling, approx 4in (10cm) in diameter for large ladybug and 2in (5cm) in diameter for the small one

❷ Either toy stuffing or a mixture of PVC bean bag granules and lavender to fill

❷ Darning needle

❷ Sewing needle

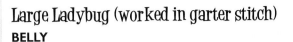

Large Ladybug (worked in garter stitch)

BELLY

**Using US 5 (3.75mm) needles and yarn A, cast on 5 sts.

Row 1: knit.

Row 2: cast on three stitches, k to end of row. (8 sts)

Row 3: cast on three stitches, k to end of row. (11 sts)

Work 2 rows straight in garter stitch without increasing.

Row 6: cast on three stitches, k to end of row. (14 sts)

Row 7: cast on three stitches, k to end of row. (17 sts)

Work 4 rows straight in garter stitch without increasing.

Row 12: cast on two stitches, k to end of row. (19 sts)

Row 13: cast on two stitches, k to end of row. (21 sts)

Work 5 rows straight in garter stitch without increasing.

Row 19: inc1 at either end of row. (23 sts)

Work 7 rows straight in garter stitch without increasing.

Row 27: k2tog at either end of row. (21 sts)**

Work 5 rows straight in garter stitch without decreasing.

Row 33: bind (cast) off two stitches, k to end of row. (19 sts)

Row 34: bind (cast) off two stitches, k to end of row. (17 sts)

Work 4 rows straight in garter stitch without decreasing.

Row 39: bind (cast) off three stitches, k to end of row. (14 sts)

Row 40: bind (cast) off three stitches, k to end of row. (11 sts)

Work 2 rows straight in garter stitch without decreasing.

Row 43: bind (cast) off three stitches, k to end of row. (8 sts)

Row 44: bind (cast) off three stitches, k to end of row. (5 sts)

Row 45: knit.

Bind (cast) off all sts.

BACK

Work as for Belly from ** to **.

Change to yarn B and work the rest of the Back same as the Belly in but using yarn B.

Small ladybug (worked in garter stitch)

BELLY

**Using US 5 (3.75mm) needles and yarn A, cast on 3 sts.

Row 1: knit.

Row 2: cast on three stitches, k to end of row. (6 sts)

Row 3: cast on three stitches, k to end of row. (9 sts)

Work 2 rows straight in garter stitch without increasing.

Row 6: cast on two stitches, k to end of row. (11 sts)

Row 7: cast on two stitches, k to end of row. (13 sts)

Work 4 rows straight in garter stitch without increasing.

Row 12: inc one stitch at either end of row. (15 sts)

Work 5 rows straight in garter stitch without increasing.

Row 18: dec one stitch at either end of row. (13 sts)**

Work 4 rows straight in garter stitch without decreasing.

Row 23: bind (cast) off two stitches, k to end of row. (11 sts)

Row 24: bind (cast) off two stitches, k to end of row. (9 sts)

Work 2 rows straight in garter stitch without decreasing.

Row 27: bind (cast) off three stitches, k to end of row. (6 sts)

Row 28: bind (cast) off three stitches, k to end of row. (3 sts)

Row 29: knit.

Bind (cast) off all three stitches.

BACK

Work as for Belly from ** to **.

Change to yarn B and work the rest of the Back same as the Belly in but using yarn B.

FINISHING

If using lavender/beanbag granules:

Sew together two circles of fabric, around edge, leaving a small gap of about ½in (1cm).

Turn pouch inside out and, using a funnel, fill with the lavender and/or beanbag granules to desired fullness.

Sew up gap.

Place pouch on Belly piece, then lay the Back on top of it and sew together knitted pieces all round edge, using darning needle and yarn A, trapping the pouch.

IF USING TOY STUFFING:

Sew together Belly and Back pieces all round edge using darning needle and yarn A, leaving a gap of about ½in (1cm). Stuff bug with toy stuffing through this opening, then sew up gap.

Skill Level

Rainbow Pillow

If you want a fun and easy way to learn how to shape your knitting, look no further than this simple pattern. Each zigzagged stripe is a single strip of knitting that is worked by simply increasing and decreasing.

MEASUREMENTS

- One size, finished cushion is approx 12 x 12in (30 x 30cm)

SKILL LEVEL

- Intermediate

YARN

- 1 x 1¾oz (50g)—approx 127yd (116m)—of Sublime Cashmere Merino Silk DK, 75% extra fine merino, 20% silk, 5% cashmere, in each of:
- **Yarn A**: shade 119 lido
- **Yarn B**: shade 124 splash
- **Yarn C**: shade 194 seesaw
- **Yarn D**: shade 195 puzzle
- **Yarn E**: shade 122 honeybunny
- **Yarn F**: shade 158 ladybug
- **Yarn G**: shade td53 purple

ALTERNATIVE YARNS

- Any DK or sportweight yarn will achieve the same size cushion, although you could use any weight of yarn and the cushion will simply come out a different size, so you will have to hold off buying the cushion pad until it is finished. Always buy a cushion pad slightly larger than your piece of fabric, so that the fabric stretches over it—there is nothing worse than a floppy cushion!

GAUGE (TENSION)

- 22 sts and 28 rows to 4in (10cm) in stockinette (stocking) stitch using US 6 (4mm) needles

NOTIONS

- Pair of US 6 (4mm) needles
- Darning needle
- 12 x 12in (30 x 30cm) cushion pad

STRIP 1

Using US 6 (4mm) needles and yarn A, cast on 6 sts.

Row 1 (RS): knit.

Row 2: purl.

**Row 3: k2, inc1, k to last two sts, inc1, k2.

Row 4: purl.

 Repeat rows 3–4 until you have 16 sts, ending with a purl row.

Next row: k2, k2tog, k to last four sts, k2tog, k2.

Next row: purl.

 Repeat last two rows until you have 6 sts, ending with a purl row.**

 Repeat from ** to ** eight more times, so you have nine full repeats.

 Bind (cast) off all sts.

 Make three more strips, one in each of yarns C, E, and G.

STRIP 2

Using US 6 (4mm) needles, and yarn B, cast on 16 sts.

Row 1 (RS): knit.

Row 2: purl.

**Row 3: k2, k2tog, k to last four sts, k2tog, k2.

Row 4: purl.

 Repeat rows 3–4 until you have 6 sts, ending with a purl row.

Next row: k2, inc1, k to last two sts, inc1, k2.

Next row: purl.

Repeat last two rows until you have 16 sts, ending with a purl row.**

Repeat from ** to ** eight more times, so you have nine full repeats.

Bind (cast) off all sts.

Make two more strips, one in each of yarns D and F.

FINISHING

Lay out all strips in alphabetical order A to G and with the right side facing down. Sew all strips together on the back with whip stitch, so that the zigzags fit together and the top and bottom are straight.

Fold around a cushion pad and sew up the three side seams.

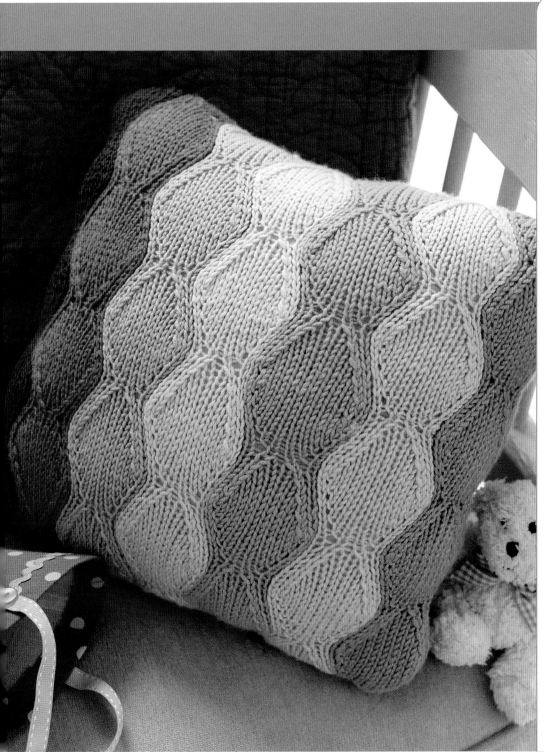

Playtime

- Doctor's stethoscope
- Stripey ball
- Candy bonbons
- Cakes and treats
- Sheriff's badge
- Teddy bear
- Beard and moustache
- Alien
- Rag doll

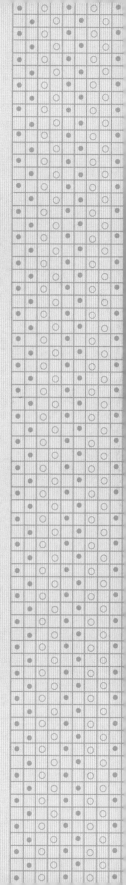

Skill Level

Doctor's Stethoscope

Make yourself a French-knitted stethoscope for dressing up as a doctor and check that all your toys are in the best of health!

MEASUREMENTS
- ❶ One size

SKILL LEVEL
- ❶ Easy

YARN
- ❶ 1 x 1¾oz (50g)—approx 127yd (116m)—of Sublime Cashmere Merino Silk DK, 75% extra fine merino, 20% silk, 5% cashmere, in shade td53 purple

YARN ALTERNATIVES
- ❶ Any yarn will do, but a DK weight will create the

same size tubes as here. Try inserting pipe cleaners into the tube to bend the stethoscope into shapes

GAUGE (TENSION)
- ❶ Not necessary

NOTIONS
- ❶ French knitting bobbin
- ❶ Darning needle
- ❶ Large button

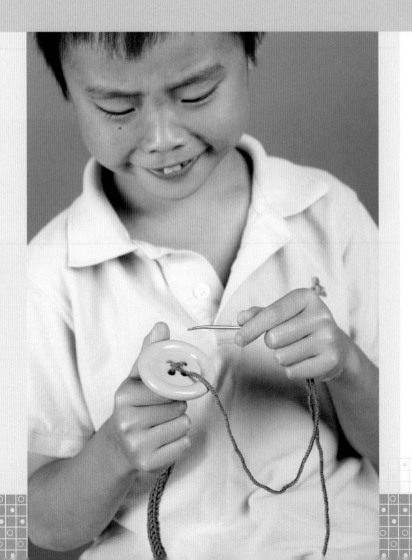

Following the instructions included with the bobbin, French knit two tubes, one 8in (20cm) long and one 16in (40cm) long.

Fold the longer one into a "U" shape and sew the shorter tube to the center bottom of the "U" tube.

Sew the large button to the bottom of the short tube.

Sew a loop of yarn to either end of the "U" tube to fit over your ears.

Skill Level

Stripey Ball

Hours of fun can be had with this easy-to-make ball. Make three and learn to juggle with them, make up a throwing and catching game, or see who can throw them the furthest (outdoors, of course!). You can stuff them with toy stuffing, or for more weight when juggling, fill with beans or beanbag granules.

MEASUREMENTS

• One size, approx 12in (30cm) around widest part

SKILL LEVEL

• Intermediate

YARN

• 1 x 1¾oz (50g)—approx 137yd (125m)—Millamia Merino, 100% merino, in each of:

• **Yarn A:** shade 140 scarlet

• **Yarn B:** shade 141 grass

• **Yarn C:** shade 144 peacock

YARN ALTERNATIVES

• Any DK weight yarn will do here to create balls of the same dimensions a these, but use thicker yarn if you want a more football-shaped ball, or thinner yarn for smaller juggling balls

GAUGE (TENSION)

• 22 sts and 30 rows to 4in (10cm) in stockinette (stocking) stitch using US 5 (3.75mm) needles

NOTIONS

• Pair of US 5 (3.75mm) needles

• Darning needle

• Toy stuffing or beanbag granules

Using US 5 (3.75mm) needles and yarn A, cast on 3 sts.

Row 1: inc1, k1, inc1. (5 sts)

Row 2: purl.

Row 3: inc1, k to last st, inc1. (7 sts)

Row 4: purl.

Row 5: inc1, k to last st, inc1. (9 sts)

  Work 3 rows st st.

Row 9: inc1, k to last st, inc1. (11 sts)

  Work 5 rows st st.

Row 15: inc1, k to last st, inc1. (13 sts)

  Work 15 rows st st.

Row 31: k2tog, k to last 2 sts, k2tog. (11 sts)

  Work 5 rows st st.

Row 37: k2tog, k to last 2 sts, k2tog. (9 sts)

  Work 3 rows st st.

Row 41: k2tog, k to last 2 sts, k2tog. (7 sts)

Row 42: purl.

Row 43: k2tog, k to last 2 sts, k2tog. (5 sts)

Row 44: purl.

Row 45: k2tog, k1, k2tog. (3 sts)

Bind (cast) off all sts.

Make one more segment in yarn A and 2 segments in each of yarns B and C: six segments in total.

Sew all six segments together, with no colors the same next to each other, all along the long sides, leaving the last seam half sewn. Fill ball with toy stuffing and/or beans to desired fullness and sew up gap.

Skill Level

Candy Bonbons

These sweet treats will look delicious piled up in a bowl in your bedroom and will make cute gifts for your friends.

MEASUREMENTS

- One size, each sweet is approx 3¼in (8cm) from side to side

YARN

- 1 x 1¾oz (50g)—approx 137yd (125m)—Millamia Merino, 100% merino, in each of:
- **Yarn A:** shade 141 grass
- **Yarn B:** shade 143 fuchsia
- **Yarn C:** shade 144 peacock
- 1 x 1¾oz (50g)—approx 131yd (120m)—Rico Essentials Merino DK, 100% merino wool, in:
- **Yarn D:** shade 64 lime

YARN ALTERNATIVES

- Any DK weight yarn will do, but a specific gauge (tension) is not essential. You could try any yarn and the sweets will just come out different sizes. You could also try some metallic yarns for sparkle, or stripe up the colors for different patterns.

GAUGE (TENSION)

- 22 sts and 28 rows to 4in (10cm) in stockinette (stocking) stitch using US 6 (4mm) needles

NOTIONS

- Pair of US 6 (4mm) needles
- Darning needle
- Sewing needle and thread
- Toy stuffing
- Assorted narrow ribbons for decoration

Using US 6 (4mm) needles and choice of yarn color, cast on 29 sts.
Row 1 (RS): knit.
Row 2: purl.
Rep rows 1–2 twice more.
Row 7: k1, [yo, k2tog] to end of row.
Work 7 rows st st, beginning with a purl row.
Next row: k1, [k2tog] to end of row. (15 sts)
Work 9 rows st st, beginning with a purl row.
Next row: k1, [inc1] to end of row. (29 sts)
Work 7 rows st st, beginning with a purl row.

Next row: k1, [yo, k2tog] to end of row.

Work 6 rows st st, beginning with a purl row.

Bind off (cast off) all sts.

FINISHING

Fold back one end of strip along row of holes (this line will want to fold automatically), and sew into place to make a scallopped hem. Do the same with opposite end.

Sew up side seam of sweet.

Using a darning needle. thread a length of yarn in and out of the stitches along the line of one hem, pull tight and tie to secure. Stuff the middle of the sweet with toy stuffing, then thread another length of yarn in and out of the stitches along the line of the other hem and pull tight to trap toy stuffing in.

Tie ribbon into small bows around each gathered end.

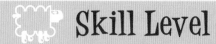 ## Skill Level

Cakes and Treats

Knitting that is good enough to eat—
almost! Fool your friends with fake food,
have a dolls' tea party, or use the cakes
as pincushions

MEASUREMENTS

One size

- **Donut** approx 4in (10cm)
in diameter
- **Sponge** approx 2¾in
(7cm) diameter
- **Cupcake** approx 2¾in
(7cm) diameter

SKILL LEVEL

- Easy

YARN

Cakes

- 1 x 1¾oz (50g)—approx
137yd (125m)—Millamia
Merino, 100% merino, in
each of:

- **Yarn A:** shade 160 fawn
- **Yarn B:** shade 143 fuchsia
- **Yarn C:** shade 162 plum
- **Yarn D:** shade 123 lilac
blossom
- 1 x 1¾oz (50g)—approx
131yd (120m)—Rico
Essentials Merino DK, 100%
merino wool, in:
- **Yarn E:** shade 10 magenta

YARN ALTERNATIVES

- Any DK weight yarn will
do here, but as a specific
gauge (tension) is not
essential you could try any
yarn and the cakes will just
come out different sizes.

GAUGE (TENSION)

- 25 sts and 32 rows to 4in
(10cm) in stockinette
(stocking) stitch using US 5
(3.75mm) needles

NOTIONS

- Pair each of US 5
(3.75mm) needles
- Darning needle
- Sewing needle and thread
- Cardboard
- Beads and buttons for
decoration
- Toy stuffing
- Felt
- French knitting doll

Donut

Using US 5 (3.75mm) needles and
yarn A, cast on 50 sts.

Row 1(RS): knit.

Row 2: purl.

Rep last two rows until work
measures approx 2¾in (7cm).

Change to yarn E and work in st st
as before for 2in (5cm).

Bind (cast) off all sts.

FINISHING

Sew cast on edge to bound (cast)
off edge and stuff resulting tube to
desired fullness with toy stuffing.

Sew tube into donut shape by
joining side seams together.

Decorate with bugle beads to
represent sprinkles.

Sponge

Using US 5 (3.75mm) needles and yarn A, cast on 40 sts.

Row 1(RS): purl.

Row 2: knit.

Work approx 2¾in (7cm) in yarn A in reverse st st as set.

Change to yarn B and work two rows reverse st st for jam filling.

Change back to A and cont in reverse st st for 2¾in (7cm).

Cut yarn but do not bind (cast) off. Thread tail through rem sts and pull up tight to gather. Secure, then sew up side seam. Insert a small circle of cardboard of approx 2¼in (6cm) in diameter to form a base then stuff the rest of cake with toy stuffing to desired fullness. Insert another circle of approx 2¼in (6cm) diameter on top of the stuffing. Using matching sewing thread, work a row of running stitches around cast-on edge and pull up to gather at top. Sew firmly closed. Sew a large red glass bead to top of sponge, over gathered center, for a cherry.

Cupcake

Using US 5 (3.75mm) needles, and yarn B, cast on 12 sts.

Row 1(RS): knit.

Row 2: purl.

Change to yarn C and work two rows st st as set.

Cont in st st working 2 rows of each color alternately until work measures approx 8in (20cm).

Bind (cast) off all sts.

Using yarn D, French-knit a length of tube approx 20in (51cm) long.

Cut a circle of felt of approx 2¼in (6cm) in diameter.

Sew cast on edge of long strip to bound-(cast-) off edge. Sew this ring to the felt circle, around the circumference.

Stuff this striped section with toy stuffing to desired fullness.

Begin to sew the French knitted tube to the top of the striped section all around the edge, winding it around on itself to create a spiral of French-knitted tube. Leave a gap unsewn at top and stuff the cone of French-knitted icing. Sew up gap.

Decorate with small round beads for sprinkles and add a large glass bead on top for a cherry, if desired.

Skill Level

Sheriff's Badge

Every town needs a sheriff to keep an eye on things, so knit yourself a star and pin it to your chest, wear it with a cowboy hat and chase the bank robbers outta town!

MEASUREMENTS

❷ One size, approx 4in (10cm) in diameter

SKILL LEVEL

❷ Easy

YARN

❷ 1 x 1¾oz (50g)—approx 137yd (125m)—Millamia Merino, 100% merino, in shade 142 daisy yellow

❷ Scraps of yarn for embroidery

YARN ALTERNATIVES

❷ Any DK weight yarn will do here as gauge (tension) is not essential. You could try any yarn and the star will just come out different sizes. You could also try some metallic yarns to make it look like a real metal star

GAUGE (TENSION)

❷ 24 sts and 30 rows to 4in (10cm) in stockinette (stocking) stitch using US 5 (3.75mm) needles

NOTIONS

❷ Pair of US 5 (3.75mm) needles

❷ Darning needle

❷ Toy stuffing

❷ Sewing needle and thread

❷ Safety pin or brooch back

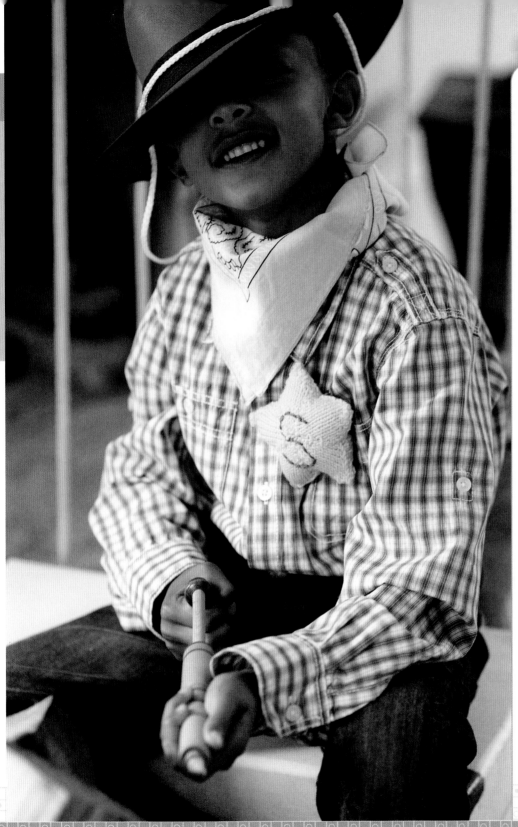

Using US 5 (3.75mm) needles, cast on 3 sts.

Next row: inc1, k to last st, inc1.

Next row: purl.

Rep last two rows until there are 11 sts, ending with a p row.

Next row: k2tog, k to last 2 sts, k2tog.

Next row: purl.

Rep last two rows until 3 sts rem, ending with a p row.

Next row: k3tog.

Fasten off yarn.

Make 9 more pieces the same, 10 pieces in total.

Sew 5 pieces together in a circle, butting the lower sides of the diamond-shapes together. Do the same with the other 5 pieces.

Wrong sides facing, sew the two stars together leaving a small gap.

Stuff star with toy stuffing to desired fullness.

Sew up gap.

Using contrast yarn, embroider an "S" onto front of star with simple straight stitches.

Sew brooch back to back of star.

Skill Level

Teddy Bear

Everyone has a favorite toy and this cute teddy is bound to become yours with his smiley little face and squishy body.

MEASUREMENTS

❶ One size, approz 11in (28cm) high

SKILL LEVEL

❶ Intermediate

YARN

❶ 1 x 1¾oz (50g)—approx 137yd (125m)—of Regia Softy, 39% new wool, 61% polyamide, in shade 435 beige

ALTERNATIVE YARNS

❶ Any DK or sportweight yarn will achieve the same size teddy, but you could try other weights and your teddy will just come out bigger or smaller. Here, the yarn is a furry, textured yarn that is incredibly soft and cozy, but you could experiment with other textures, although using a machine washable yarn is a good idea so that when you have played with and hugged teddy so much that he is grubby, it is easy to make him as good as new.

GAUGE (TENSION)

❶ 24 sts and 32 rows to 4in (10cm) in stockinette (stocking) stitch using US 6 (4mm) needles

NOTIONS

❶ Pair of US 6 (4mm) needles
❶ Darning needle
❶ Toy stuffing
❶ Buttons for eyes
❶ Ribbon for decoration, if desired
❶ Oddments of embroidery thread or yarn for face

Note: you can use either side of the st st as the right side on this pattern, or a mixture of both, as here, to use both textures—each looks good in this furry yarn.

LEGS

Using US 6 (4mm) needles, cast on 20 sts and work 4¼in (11cm) in st st.

Do not bind (cast) off.

Break yarn and thread through rem sts, pulling up tight. Sew side seam to form a tube and stuff leg with toy stuffing to desired fullness.

Thread yarn in and out all around cast-on edge of leg and pull up tight to close.

ARMS

Using US 6 (4mm) needles, cast on 16 sts and work 3¼in (8cm) in st st

Do not bind (cast) off.

Break yarn and thread through rem sts, pulling up tight. Sew side seam and stuff arm with toy stuffing to desired fullness.

Thread yarn in and out all around cast-on edge of arm and pull up tight to close.

BODY

Using US 6 (4mm) needles, cast on 50 sts and work 4¼in (11cm) in st st.

Do not bind (cast) off.

Break yarn and thread through rem sts, pulling up tight. Sew side seam and stuff body with toy stuffing to desired fullness.

Thread yarn in and out all around cast-on edge of body and pull up tight to close.

HEAD

Using US 6 (4mm) needles, cast on 60 sts and work 3½in (9cm) in st st.

Do not bind (cast) off.

Break yarn and thread through rem sts, pulling up tight. Sew side seam and stuff head with toy stuffing to desired fullness.

Thread yarn in and out all around cast-on edge of head and pull up tight to close.

EARS

Using US 6 (4mm) needles, cast on 9 sts.

Knit one row.

Next row: k2tog, k to last 2 sts, k2tog.

Rep last two rows until 5 sts rem.

Knit one row.

Bind (cast) off all sts.

FINISHING

Sew head and limbs to body.

Sew ears to head, along with buttons for eyes and embroider on a mouth and nose.

Tie ribbon around teddy's neck, if desired.

Skill Level

Beard and Moustache

These fake facial hairpieces are the perfect disguise for playing at being a spy, or for fancy dress! You do not have to stick to natural hair colors—try mad brights!

MEASUREMENTS

- ● One size

SKILL LEVEL

- ● Intermediate

YARN

Beard

- ● 1 x 1¾oz (50g)—approx 169yd (155m)—of Regia Pompon 43% wool, 37% polyamide, 18% polyester, in shade 275

Moustache

- ● 1 x 1¾oz (50g)—approx 114yd (105m)—of Wendy Allegra, 32% Alpaca, 31% acrylic, 37% polyester, in shade 957

GAUGE (TENSION)

- ● Not necessary

NOTIONS

- ● Pair each of US 10 (6mm) and US 4 (3.5mm) needles
- ● Darning needle

Beard

Using US 4 (3.5mm) needles, cast on 20 sts.

Working in garter st (every row knit), inc1 at start of every other row until you have 26 sts.

Work straight in garter st for 1¼in (3cm), ending at straight side.

Next row: k5, bind (cast) off two sts for mouth, k to end.

Work in garter stitch on these 19 sts for 1¼in (3cm), ending at mouth edge.

Rejoin yarn to 5 unworked sts and work in garter st on these 5 sts until piece measures same as worked side of mouth, ending at mouth edge.

Cast on 2 sts over mouth, k to end of row. (26 sts).

Work straight on these sts for 1¼in (3cm) ending at straight side, then k2tog at end of next and every other row until 20 sts rem.

Bind (cast) off all sts.

Finger-knit two lengths of chain of approx 20in (51cm) and attach one to either side of top edge of beard to tie beard on.

Moustache

Using US 10 (6mm) needles, cast on 12 sts.

Working in garter st (every row knit), inc1 at either end of next 2 rows. (16 sts)

Cast on 8 sts at end of next row.

Bind (cast) off these same 8 sts at beg of next row and cast on 8 more at the end of next row.

Bind (cast) off all sts.

Finger-knit two lengths of chain (see page 41) approx 20in (50cm) long and attach one to either thick side of moustache to tie moustache on.

Roll thin ends of moustache up and allow to sit twisted as with a real "curled-at-the-ends" moustache.

Skill Level

Alien

Cute and weird alien toys made out of fur yarn can be embellished in many ways to create unique little critters.

MEASUREMENTS

❂ One size, approx 8in (20cm) tall

SKILL LEVEL

❂ Intermediate

YARN

❂ **Yarn A:** 1 x 1¾oz (50g)— approx 71yd (65m)—Sirdar Escape Wool Rich Chunky, 51% wool, 49% acrylic, in shade 197

❂ **Yarn B:** 1 x 1¾oz (50g)— approx 43yd (40m)—Gedifra Antiga, 34% acrylic, 30% polyamide, 18% mohair, 18% wool, in shade 3101

ALTERNATIVE YARNS

❂ Any bulky weight yarn can be used to replicate this alien; as gauge (tension) is not important, the toy will just vary in size. You could also try knitting it all in a fur yarn, or all in a regular yarn

GAUGE (TENSION)

❂ 10 sts and 14 rows to 4in (10cm) in garter stitch using US 11 (8mm) needles

NOTIONS

❂ Pair of US 11 (8mm) needles
❂ Darning needle
❂ Toy stuffing
❂ Buttons for eyes
❂ Felt for limbs

Using yarn A and US 11 (8mm) needles, cast on 12 sts.

Row 1: knit.

Row 2: inc1, k to last st, inc1. (14 sts)

Rep last 2 rows until you have 22 sts.

Work straight in garter st until work measures 3¼in (8cm) from cast on edge.

Change to yarn B and work 2in (5cm) in garter st.

Next row: k2tog, k to last 2 sts, k2tog. (20 sts)

Next row: knit.

Rep last 2 rows once more. (18 sts)

Cont on these 18 sts for 1¼in (3cm).

Next row: k4, turn, leaving rem sts unworked.

Work 4 rows garter st on these 4 sts.

Next row: [k2tog] twice. (2 sts)

Next row: knit.

Next row: k2tog, fasten off yarn.

Rejoin yarn to rem 14 sts, k5, turn, leaving rem sts unworked.

Work 4 rows garter st on these 5 sts.

Next row: k2tog, k1, k2tog. (3 sts)

Next row: knit.

Next row: k3tog, fasten off yarn.

Rejoin yarn to rem 9 sts, k5, turn, leaving rem sts unworked.

Work 4 rows garter st on these 5 sts.

Next row: k2tog, k1, k2tog. (3 sts)

Next row: knit.

Next row: k3tog, fasten off yarn.

Rejoin yarn to rem 4 sts, k4.

Work 4 further rows garter st on these 4 sts.

Next row: [k2tog] twice. (2 sts)

Next row: knit.

Next row: k2tog, fasten off yarn.

Make one more piece in the same way.

FINISHING

Cut out four felt triangles for arms and four slightly larger felt triangles for legs.

Sew the arm pieces together, leaving one seam open for stuffing. Fill with toy stuffing to desired fullness and sew up gap.

Sew two body pieces together, inserting the arms and legs in position and sewing in place as you go. Leave a small gap for stuffing.

Fill with toy stuffing to desired fullness and sew up gap.

Attach eyes to the yarn A section of alien. You can also embroider a mouth and any other weird or scary features you want.

Rag Doll

It is easy to make your little rag doll different from everyone else's by changing her hair color—perhaps to match your own or even a fun, bright shade. You can sew on different features for her face or add sewn fabric clothes or pockets. Have fun!

MEASUREMENTS

● One size, approx 23in (58.5cm) tall

SKILL LEVEL

● Difficult

YARN

● 1 x 1¾oz (50g)—approx 91yd (84m)—Crystal Palace Cotton Twirl Solids, 90% cotton 10% nylon, in each of:

● **Yarn A:** shade 2929 mango

● **Yarn B:** shade 2905 concord grape

● **Yarn C:** shade 2927 calypso

● **Yarn D:** shade 2907 lime juice

GAUGE (TENSION)

● 18 sts and 24 rows to 4in (10cm) in stockinette (stocking) stitch using US 7 (4.5mm) needles

NOTIONS

● Pair of US 7 (4.5mm) needles

● Darning needle

● Toy stuffing

● Scraps of felt for cheeks

● Sewing needle and thread

● Buttons for eyes and for dress

BODY

Using US 7 (4.5mm) needles and yarn A, cast on 40 sts.

Work 5½in (14cm) in st st.

Bind (cast) off all sts.

Fold piece in half widthways and sew up two of the seams. Fill the body with toy stuffing to desired fullness then sew up the remaining seam.

HEAD

Using US 7 (4.5mm) needles and yarn A, cast on 12 sts.

Row 1: knit.

Row 2: purl.

Row 3: inc1, k to last st, inc1. (14 sts)

Row 4: purl.

Rep last two rows until you have 24 sts, ending with a row 4

Cont in st st without increasing for 8 rows, ending with a p row.

Next row: k2tog, k to last 2 sts, k2tog. (22 sts)

Next row: purl.

Rep last two rows until you have 12 sts.

Bind (cast) off all sts.

Make one more piece the same, but using yarn B.

Sew two pieces together all round edge, with yarn B piece as back of head with purl side as right side and yarn A piece as face with knit side as right side. Leave a small gap for stuffing. Fill with toy stuffing to desired fullness and sew up gap.

ARMS (MAKE TWO)

Using US 7 (4.5mm) needles and yarn A, cast on 6 sts.

Work 5½in (14cm) in st st.

Bind (cast) off all sts.

Fold piece in half widthways and sew up one short seam and the long seam. Fill the arm with toy stuffing to desired fullness then sew up the remaining short seam.

LEGS (MAKE TWO)

Using US 7 (4.5mm) needles and yarn B, cast on 11 sts.

Work in st st for two rows.

Change to yarn C and work 2 rows st st.

Cont straight in st st in this way, working stripes as established until legs measure 12in (30cm).

Bind (cast) off all sts.

Fold piece in half widthways and sew up one short seam and the long seam. Fill the leg with toy stuffing to desired fullness then sew up the remaining short seam.

BODY FINISHING

Sew head, arms, and legs to body, with arms approx ½in (1cm) down from the top of body and legs attached to bottom seam of body.

DRESS

Using US 7 (4.5mm) needles and yarn D, cast on 28 sts.

Working in st st, k2tog at either end of 7th and every foll 8th row until 20 sts remain.

Cont straight until work measures 6¼in (16cm).

Bind (cast) off all sts.

Make one more piece the same.

Sew dress pieces together, around the body, leaving holes in the side seams for the arms and in center of top seam for head.

POCKET

Using US 7 (4.5mm) needles and yarn C, cast on 9 sts.

Row 1: purl.

Row 2: inc1, k to last st, inc1. (11 sts)

Rep last two rows once more. (13 sts)

Work 5 rows st st.

Bind (cast) off all sts.

Sew to dress front using yarn B. Sew on buttons.

HAIR PLAITS

Cut 12 lengths of yarn B 49in (124cm) long. Keeping the strands in a bunch, safety pin the mid point to the center of your doll's head. Using yarn C, attach the tassel by sewing around the hair at the top corners of your doll's head. Remove the safety pin. Spilt one side of the tassel's 12 ends into 3 sections (4 strands each section) and plait to the end, tying a knot at the bottom to secure. Repeat for the other side.

FINISHING

Sew on button eyes. Cur circles of felt and sew them on for cheeks. Embroider other features in yarn.

Abbreviations

alt	alternate		**p2tog**	purl two stitches together
beg	beginning		**patt**	pattern
cont	continue		**rem**	remaining
dec	decrease		**rep**	repeat
DK	double knitting (yarn weight)		**rev st st**	reverse stockinette (stocking) stitch
foll(s)	follow(s) (ing)			
inc1	increase		**RS**	right side
k	knit		**st(s)**	stitch(es)
k2tog	knit two stitches together		**st st**	stockinette (stocking) stitch
k3tog	knit three stitches together		**tog**	together
p	purl		**WS**	wrong side

Suppliers

USA

CRYSTAL PALACE
Love Knitting
Tel: 866-677-0057
www.loveknitting.com

DEBBIE BLISS
SIRDAR
SUBLIME
Knitting Fever Inc.
PO Box 336
315 Bayview Ave
Amityville
NY 11701
Tel: 516-546-3600
Fax: 516-546-6871
www.knittingfever.com

PATONS
Coats & Clark
Consumer Services
P.O. Box 12229
Greenville
SC 29612-0229
Tel: 800-648-1479
www.coatsandclark.com

PURL (SHOP)
459 Broome Street
New York
NY 10013
Tel: 212-420-8796
www.purlsoho.com

ROWAN YARNS
REGIA
Love Knitting
Tel: 866-677-0057
www.loveknitting.com

**DOWNTOWN YARNS
(SHOP)**
45 Avenue A
New York
NY 10009
Tel: 212-995-5991
www.downtownyarns.com

Canada

PATONS
320 Livingstone Avenue South
Listowel
Ontario N4W 3H3
Tel: 1-888-368-8401
www.spinriteyarns.com

DEBBIE BLISS
REGIA
ROWAN YARNS
SIRDAR
SUBLIME
Diamond Yarns Ltd
155 Martin Ross Avenue
Unit 3
Toronto
Ontario M3J 2L9
Tel: 416-736-6111
www.diamondyarn.com

UK

CRYSTAL PALACE

Love Knitting
7th Floor,
10 Bloomsbury Way,
London,
WC1A 2SL
Tel: 0845 544 2196
www.loveknitting.com

SIRDAR SPINNING LTD.

Flanshaw Lane
Wakefield
West Yorkshire WF2 9ND
United Kingdom
Tel: 01924 231669
www.sirdar.co.uk

DEBBIE BLISS

Designer Yarns
Unit 8-10 Newbridge Industrial
Estate
Pitt Street
Keighley
West Yorkshire BD21 4PQ
Tel: 01535 664222
Fax: 01535 664333
www.designeryarns.uk.com

MILLAMIA

Tel: 08450 177474.
exclusively available via
www.loveknitting.com

ROWAN YARNS

MEZ Crafts UK
17F
Brooke's Mill
Armitage Bridge
Huddersfield
West Yorkshire
HD4 7NR
Tel: 01484 950 630
www.knitrowan.com

PATONS

MEZ Crafts UK
17F
Brooke's Mill
Armitage Bridge
Huddersfield
West Yorkshire
HD4 7NR
Tel: 01484 950 630
www.coatscrafts.co.uk or
www.mezcrafts.co.uk

LOOP (SHOP)

15 Camden Passage
Islington
London N1 8EA
Tel: 020 7288 1160
Email: info@loopknitting.com

GET KNITTED (SHOP)

39 Brislington Hill
Brislington
Bristol BS4 5BE
Tel: 0117 3005211
www.loopknittingshop.com

International

RICO YARNS

RICO DESIGN GmbH & Co.
KG Industriestrasse 19 - 23
33034 Brakel
Germany
www.rico-design.de

BC GARN

BC Garn Aps,
Elbow 56A
DK – 6000 Kolding
Denmark
+45 75 89 73 84
www.bcgarn.dk

Acknowledgments

This has been an incredibly fun book to write, knit, and shoot and it would not have been half so much fun if it wasn't for some of the people who have helped it into being.

Firstly I must thank the models: Emilie, Reo, Alice, Jocasta, Jemima, Henry, Freddie, Billie, Tilly, Kiera, and Aiden. who were a joy to shoot and, in many cases, had us roaring with laughter, making it feel like anything but work. I cannot forget the contribution of their parents, including Mel, Marcelle, Karen, and Ling, who often patiently knitted away while we were shooting. It has been so lovely to meet so many people who are still passing the love of knitting down to their children, which is what this book is essentially about.

The team who have worked on the book have been fabulous—thanks to Martin, Terry, and Ian the photographers, who have captured the pure joy of knitting with children delightfully. Also thanks to Cindy, Pete, Sally, Elizabeth, Marilyn, and especially Kate for their support and for seeing the book's potential and allowing me realize a dream by finally publishing **Knitting for Children** and making it look so beautiful.

I am extremely grateful to all the yarn companies who donated yarn, especially to the lovely ladies at Millamia and Sublime, who are always incredibly supportive.

My undying gratitude must go to my hardworking mother, Mary, and grandmother, Patsy, and also to my friend, Clare, who have helped out with additional knitting when it all became too much for my hands to cope with.

Finally, to Sean and my family, thanks as always. They have been a fantastic support throughout the many ups and downs of writing a book, meeting deadlines, dealing with AWOL yarn and repetitive strain injuries!

Thank you to you all,

Claire

Index